Ben Norman

Getting Noticed on Google

Invaluable Tips to Increase your
Website Ranking on Google

In Easy Steps is an imprint of Computer Step
Southfield Road · Southam
Warwickshire CV47 0FB · United Kingdom
www.ineasysteps.com

Notice of liability
Every effort has been made to ensure this book contains accurate and current information. However, Computer Step and the author shall not be liable for any loss or damage suffered by readers as a result of any information contained herein.

Trademarks
All trademarks are acknowledged as belonging to their respective companies.

Thanks
I would like to thank the following people for their help, advice and services: Harshad Kotecha for writing support and Sarah Woodall for final proofreading.

Special thanks to my parents, partner, family and friends for their continual support and enabling me to get to this position.

Printed and bound in the United Kingdom

ISBN-13 978-1-84078-332-2
ISBN-10 1-84078-332-X

Contents

1 Introduction to Google

Before you start optimizing your website, you need to know who you are optimizing for. This simple introduction will get you fully acquainted with Google, the world's most popular search engine.

Welcome to Google

Google is the world's most popular search engine, receiving more daily enquiries than any other. It has become the clear leader for search on the internet, performing nearly twice as many searches as its nearest rivals.

Google first appeared in 1997 as a very simple search box. Over the years Google has retained its simplicity and has concentrated purely on making search more relevant. This is the reason for Google's massive growth and continued success.

Hot tip

To get the most relevant results when searching make sure your searches are as specific as possible.

Google has become an internet icon and in everyday conversations you will often hear people say "just Google it". This shows the massive impact that this simple search box has had on ordinary people's lives.

Google's core business is search, which it takes very seriously. This business consists of two main parts: natural search and sponsored listings.

Google, like any other business, will continue to grow and mature – an exciting future is open to the world's most popular search engine.

Google is an advertising vertical in its own right that, if used properly, can provide an abundance of highly converting traffic.

Businesses have come to learn very quickly that if their websites appear in the top search results of Google, the relevant traffic they attract will be colossal.

Any company can have their website appear in Google as long as it is deemed relevant enough. The problem most companies have is getting their websites into a position where they can be found.

How Google works

Google has an algorithm that it uses to evaluate websites to determine their relevance.

Google's algorithm has hidden criteria, like its secret blend of spices, that make the most relevant website. The algorithm will weigh up websites to see how relevant they are compared to Google's image of how the most relevant website should be. Google will score each website to determine how close it is compared with the ideal website, and rank it accordingly.

These points will be scored for details ranging from the title of the web page to the number of inward links it has pointing to it. The overall score is then assessed to see how relevant the page is for the searcher's specific search phrase. This will determine where a website will appear in the search engine's results.

To collect the information contained on websites, Google uses programs called spiders. Google's spiders will crawl the internet, moving from website to website via hyperlinks and collecting data on their travels. Google will then take the information collected on each website and decide whether it is relevant enough to be placed in its search results and, if so, where.

Google will not automatically enter every website into its search results because this would make its results less relevant, and relevance is Google's main objective.

It is in what lies beneath Google's simple search box in the algorithm they use to place websites where the real power of Google can be found.

Beware

Google's complex algorithm means that it can and will detect attempts to fool it and will penalize you.

Getting to Google's heart

To get to Google's heart and have your site appear in this search engine is not as impossible as people believe it to be.

There is one sure way to Google's heart and the top of this search engine, and that is through relevance.

Google has founded its success upon relevance, and if you follow their simple guidelines, achieving top positions is not beyond anyone's reach.

If you have a well-designed website that contains unique and relevant content, then the chances are Google will like your site.

The main reason people experience problems is that they do not effectively promote their websites to Google. Website owners often misrepresent their sites with non-descriptive titles and headings, and do not utilize the free tools available.

This costly mistake can mean the difference between a top ten placement and coming in at 129th. The first will see your traffic and profits soar and the second will ensure that your site is virtually invisible.

There is another deciding factor that Google uses to determine rank positions and this involves link building from other sites. Google will find out how many links are pointing to your website from other websites and use this information to determine relevance.

If Google finds links to your website from other relevant websites and those links use relevant keywords, Google will recognize this.

This is why linking from relevant sites is very beneficial and will increase your chances of being found in Google's search results. This has proved crucial in the growth of Google and the continued relevance of its search results.

This is why, first and foremost, when creating and maintaining your website you must ensure that it remains relevant to your topic. If you stick to this simple yet effective rule, Google will find it easier to determine the relevance of your website.

Content is what Google wants and the more relevant to your subject the better. Give Google that and top rankings are sure to follow.

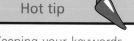

Hot tip

Keeping your keywords relevant will maximize your chances of gaining top ranking positions in Google's results.

Don't forget

Effective link building will increase your chances of a high position in Google.

Why is Google so important?

If you could be at the top of only one search engine the one to choose would be Google. The reason for this is very simple: more people use Google than any other search engine. Google receives millions of enquiries every day – missing out on the targeted traffic that passes through this search engine would be a grave mistake.

In a study of US search trends, comScore found that Google accounted for 42.7% of the searches conducted. This is nearly half the market, as you can see from the graph shown below.

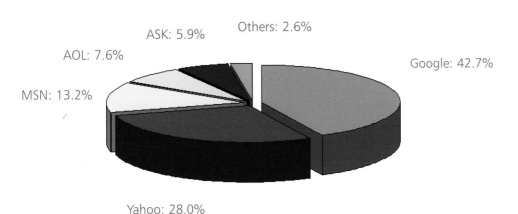

Source: comScore for searchenginewatch.com

Google's algorithm is very clever and this makes its results very difficult to bias or to cheat your way into.

People see this as reassurance that the results in Google will be very relevant to their searches. This helps people to build trust in this search engine and also to be more trusting of the websites that it displays.

This gives Google the ability to advise people on the best websites that match their specific search queries. If your website is among the top results for your niche, there is a large amount of targeted traffic that you can receive.

The best thing about this search traffic is that people landing at your website will be actively looking for your product or service, which means that you can be sure of a high conversion rate.

Don't forget

Google accounts for nearly half of the searches conducted on the internet so make sure your website is easily accessible by Google.

Why not just pay per click?

Businesses, now more than ever, are using Google to market their products and services as they realize the abundance of targeted traffic it provides.

This then poses the question: do you optimize your website to appear in Google's natural search listings or do you pay to be placed in the sponsored listings?

It can sometimes seem an easy option just to pay for results, but is it really the right decision?

In a recent study, Google found that searchers were 72% more likely to click on a natural listing rather than a pay-per-click advert. This shows that although you can pay to get your website seen at the top of Google, it is not as effective as having it appear there naturally.

Searchers look for relevance in the adverts they click on, in the same way that Google looks for relevance in the websites it shows in its natural listings. This is why natural search offers a much greater conversion rate: People know that the natural listings will tend to be more relevant to their search as they cannot be bought, only earned.

You can distinguish between Google's natural and sponsored listings as Google separates them in the following format:

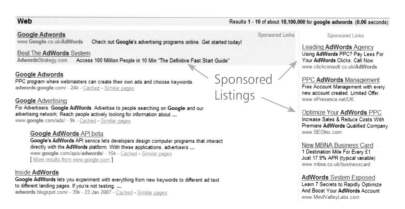

The main benefit of natural listings is that they are free to earn and maintain. There are no click prices or fees as with pay per click. This is not to say that pay per click is not worth doing, just that natural listings are deemed more relevant and cost-effective.

Don't forget

Pay per click can seem an easy and fast way to achieve results but it is not always the most cost-effective option.

Hot tip

Naturally ranked websites are more highly regarded than sponsored listings. Therefore optimizing your site using relevant keywords and a user-friendly structure will be far more beneficial and will create more targeted traffic than pay per click would.

What is organic SEO?

Organic Search Engine Optimization, or Organic SEO as it is commonly called, is the process of optimizing your website to appear higher in the search engine's natural listings.

A dictionary definition of the word "optimization" is:

"An act, process, or methodology of making something (as a design, system, or decision) as fully perfect, functional, or effective as possible; specifically: the mathematical procedures (as finding the maximum of a function) involved in this."

This is exactly what you need to do to your website to give it the prominence in the search engine that it deserves.

Search engine optimization involves the optimization of many different parts and, to optimize your website effectively, we will need to look at and optimize each of the following:

- Keywords
- Meta data
- Content
- Inward links
- Header tags
- Alt tags
- Internal links
- Website structure
- Website theme
- Website code

Once optimized, websites will stand a much greater chance of being found for their desired keywords. This is, after all, the whole reason for having a website.

There is no charge for appearing in Google's natural search engine listings, unlike other forms of advertising such as pay per click. This makes organic search engine optimization a very cost-effective method of advertising.

Hot tip

It costs nothing to appear in Google's natural search results so ensure you make the most of this free advertising method.

The world as Google sees it

Google sees the internet differently from the way searchers see it and it is important to understand this when designing your website initially and when optimizing it.

Paying attention to the coding of your website can often help when trying to find problems that are holding you back in Google.

Websites can often look fine at first glance but when you look at the world as Google sees it, by viewing the source code, you can see where the problems lie.

Website as we see it:

Web   Images   Video   News   Maps   more »

Google Search   I'm Feeling Lucky

Advanced Search
Preferences
Language Tools

Advertising Programs - Business Solutions - About Google - Go to Google UK

Make Google Your Homepage!

Website as Google sees it:

```
<html><head><meta http-equiv="content-type" content="text/html; charset=UTF-8">
body,td,a,p,.h{font-family:arial,sans-serif}
.h{font-size:20px}
.h{color:#3366cc}
.q{color:#00c}
--></style>
<script defer>
<!--
function sf(){document.f.q.focus();}
window.clk=function(b,c,d,h,i,j){if(document.images){var a=window.encodeURIComp
</script>
</head><body bgcolor=#ffffff text=#000000 link=#0000cc vlink=#551a8b alink=#ff0
function qs(el){if(window.RegExp&&window.encodeURIComponent){var ue=el.href,qe=
function togDisp(e){stopB(e);var elems=document.getElementsByName('more');for(v
function stopB(e){if(!e)e=window.event;e.cancelBubble=true;}
document.onclick=function(event){var elems=document.getElementsByName('more');i
//-->
</script><table border=0 cellspacing=0 cellpadding=4><tr><td nowrap><font size=
.cb{margin:.5ex}
--></style>
<span name=more id=more style="display:none;position:absolute;background:#fff;b
```

This is why it is important that, when your website is designed, it is done in such a way that the page will validate (see page 52) – so that it looks good to searchers and to Google. This will in turn make it easier for Google to crawl your website.

Google takes information from your website code, not from the images we see, to assess your website. This is why it is important to ensure that your website code validates so that Google can find the information it needs.

Hot tip

When optimizing your website, view it as Google sees it – look at the source code – as this can make it easier to identify any errors in the coding.

Hot tip

To view the source code select View from the toolbar and then select Source.

Google's data centers

Google has many different data centers dotted around the globe that it uses to store copies of the web pages in its index. This means that at any time you could be querying any one of Google's data centers.

You will usually query the data center that is geographically closest to you but this will be dependant on traffic and, if one of the centers is under excessive load, your query may be passed on to one of the others.

Google also has two test domains that it will use to test its new algorithms before they are accepted and rolled out across the real data centers. It can be handy to keep an eye on these, as you can see how your website would be placed if the new algorithm were rolled out.

There are many free tools on the internet that you can use to query the different data centers to see what your rankings are on each of them.

One of these tools is available at:

http://www.seochat.com/seo-tools/multiple-datacenter-google-search/

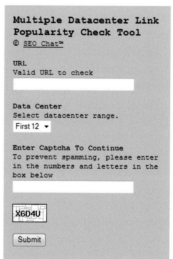

1 Enter keywords

2 Enter captcha code

3 Click Submit

You can use this to see when Google is performing updates, as changes are slowly rolled out across the data centers. This means that at times of updates you will see a variety of results.

Ethical optimization

There are two ways of optimizing your website to appear higher in the search engine's natural listings, the ethical way and the unethical way.

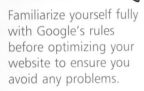
These are also known as "white hat SEO" and "black hat SEO". We will only cover the ethical way, using white hat SEO, as this is the only sustainable, long-term optimization technique.

To optimize using unethical methods can seem an attractive proposition as the results can be gained quickly, but these are often short-lived. The minute that Google realizes what you are doing, your website will be removed and your domain blacklisted.

This can cause unmeasurable damage to your business as studies have shown that Google can hold it against the domain indefinitely. This could mean you would have to start with a new domain name and new website.

It is important that when you are optimizing your website for Google you adhere to some simple ethical rules to ensure that what you're doing is not against Google's code of practice. This will avoid future problems and ensure that everything that you do will be helping your ranking and not harming your site.

It is important to familiarize yourself with Google's webmaster guidelines as they will help you ensure you are not breaking any rules. These rules can be found on Google's home page by navigating to the About Google section. Once you have familiarized yourself with Google's guidelines, you will be in a much better position to decide on the ethical approach you wish to take to market your site with Google's rules in mind.

It is very important that when optimizing websites you only use ethical search engine optimization and stay away from so called "black hat SEO" techniques. Using black hat techniques will eventually prove beneficial to no one. Potential clients will be drawn to your site under false pretences, believing your site to contain content relevant to their specific search, but when arriving at your site will find this information non-existent.

This is the reason Google will penalize you for using such activities: the site would be irrelevant and so would jeopardize the quality of the search results.

2 Free essential tools and services

To help Google find and place your website we are going to use a number of free tools. We will introduce you to these tools in this chapter.

The Google toolbar

The Google toolbar is a free search bar like many others available on the web but this one has some features that are worth their weight in gold.

The Google toolbar is positioned at the top of your browser and will give you valuable information about the website you are viewing.

Google's toolbar also acts as a search tool that is always available to you so, regardless of where you are on the web, you can start a new search without having to navigate to the Google homepage.

The Google toolbar is jam-packed full of useful features including:

- AutoFill
- AutoLink
- Translate
- Pop-up blocker
- Spell checker
- PageRank display
- Highlight search terms
- Word find buttons
- Bookmarks
- Send to
- Google account sign-in
- Gmail access
- Automatic update facility
- Optional privacy and security features

Don't forget

When you want to perform a search just use your Google toolbar – it will save you having to navigate to a search engine.

Hot tip

Do not worry about buying a pop-up blocker: with the Google toolbar you get it for free.

Download the Google toolbar

1 Click About Google on the Google homepage

2 Select Google Services & Tools

Don't forget

To use the PageRank facility you must enable the feature in your privacy settings.

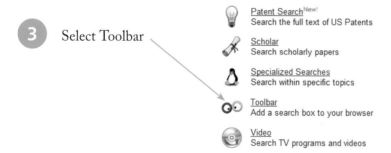

3 Select Toolbar

4 Click Download Google Toolbar

Backward link checker

The main and most valuable feature of the Google toolbar is its backward link checker. A backward link is simply a link that comes into your website from another website.

1 Navigate to your website and right-click on the main page. Then select Page Info>Backward Links

Using your backward link checker you will be able to:

● See who links to your website

● Assess the quality of the links

● Find out who your competition are

● See who links to your competition and how

● Source new links for your website

The Google toolbar makes finding out the answers to these questions easy by giving you a browser-based interface that is present every time you go online.

This means that you can simply navigate to your own website, or a competitor's website, and hit the backward link button to find out who is linking to the site.

Once you have found a page that links to the site, you can even navigate to that page and find out even more information including:

● The PageRank of the website the link is on

● The anchor text used for the link

● Whether you can get a link from the page

This is a great benefit. Without this tool the process of assessing and finding incoming links would be much more difficult and time consuming.

Cached pages checker

Another very helpful tool when working out how you are faring in the optimization of your website is the Google cached page feature.

Hot tip

You can also check your cached pages using the button on the toolbar.

With this simple tool you can, at the touch of a button, find out exactly how Google sees your web page and when it was last crawled and cached.

The cached page checker shows you how Google sees a web page as it was when it last visited the website. It is important to note that the displayed image of a page may be different from the image we see. This may happen if cascading style sheets (CSS) were used to arrange items on the page. Google will only be interested in the content, and that is what it displays.

You can use this tool to check whether Google has noticed the changes you have made to the website and whether it has updated its cache.

If you have made changes to your website and the cached page tool is showing your old page it would indicate that Google has not yet updated and you should wait before you make any further alterations.

If Google has updated its cache but you are still not seeing effective results, this would indicate that Google doesn't think the changes make any difference to the site's relevance.

This tool will make sure that you do not overwrite your changes erroneously and will take the guesswork out of changing your website.

Beware

Before making further changes to your website ensure that Google has your most recent website in its cache.

Google account

If you want to use many of the Google tools and features then you will need to have a Google account.

Login screen

Don't forget

You will need a Google account to take advantage of the free tools and services.

A Google account will offer you the ability to use and sign up for the following relevant services:

- Froogle
- AdWords
- AdSense
- Sitemaps
- Google Alerts
- Google Groups
- Analytics
- Personalized Search

Once your Google account has been activated, you will be able to access and utilize any of the tools you have signed up for. This is convenient as you will have one login that can be used for all of the tools.

This enables you to access all of your Google tools and services from one easy-to-manage account.

To get your free Google account and gain access to all of the previously mentioned tools and services, follow the steps below:

1 Type "google account" into the Google search box

2 Select the Google Accounts link

Don't forget

Your Google account will enable you to access all services via one login.

3 Click "Create an account now"

4 Enter your details and click "I accept" at the bottom of the form

Google sitemaps

Hot tip

To learn how to create a sitemap and upload it to Google, see page 95.

If you want to help yourself and at the same time help Google, then you need to get a Google sitemap.

Hot tip

Use Google sitemaps to find out the problem areas of your website.

Having a Google sitemap will offer you many great benefits. It will help you with:

- Understanding Google's view of your site

- Diagnosing potential problems with your website

- Seeing how Google crawls and indexes your website

- Monitoring the performance of your website

- Learning what search phrases bring traffic to your website

- Sharing information with Google to help it better index your website

This is one of Google's most useful tools. It enables you to tell Google when you have changed your website and what you have done to it. This means you will have more control over how quickly Google re-crawls your website after you make changes to it.

The other great feature is that Google will feed back to you crucial information about your website and its visitors, helping you further increase the effectiveness of your website.

Google Analytics

If you would like to see how searchers are visiting your website, where they are coming from and how often they visit, then it's your lucky day. You can find out all of this and more by signing up to a free Google Analytics account, which gives you all the benefits of an advanced website statistics program.

Sophisticated. Easy. Free.

Google Analytics tells you everything you want to know about how your visitors found you and how they interact with your site. Focus your marketing resources on campaigns and initiatives that deliver ROI, and improve your site to convert more visitors.

Integrated with AdWords.

Google Analytics has the enterprise level capabilities you'd expect from a high end web analytics offering and also provides timesaving integration with AdWords. Of course, Google Analytics tracks all of your non-AdWords initiatives as well.

Learn more >>

Sign Up Now. »

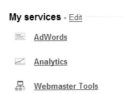

Hot tip

Google Analytics can tell you exactly what your visitors are doing on your website, and it's free.

Signing up with the Google Analytics service will enable you to find out lots of information regarding your site and its visitors.

To sign up to Google Analytics for free just follow the steps below:

1 Log in to your Google account and click Analytics from the services menu

My services - Edit

   AdWords

   Analytics

   Webmaster Tools

2 Click on the Sign Up button

Sign Up for Google Analytics

You are just a few steps from Google Analytics. Click on the Sign Up button to get started.

Sign Up »

3 Enter the details requested and click Continue

Once you have signed up and installed the tracking code, Google will start to track your website and feed back valuable information that will enable you to optimize your site more effectively.

Web ceo

When you are optimizing websites you can do it yourself, although it is always better to get a helping hand.

There is a piece of software available to download that will offer you lots of help with the process of optimizing and analyzing your website.

We will be using this software to assist you and make your life easier. This software is available as a free download for website owners to use on their own sites. This service is completely free with no ongoing charges or fees to pay.

There is of course a full version, which you can buy if you are planning on optimizing lots of sites or doing it as a profession.

Web ceo also offers a free training program and certificate to everyone who downloads this software so you really have nothing to lose and everything to gain.

Web ceo is jam-packed full of useful features including:

- Keyword research
- Search engine optimization
- Link popularity analyzer
- PPC campaigns manager
- Ranking checker
- Web analytics

To get your free copy of this software visit the website at www.webceo.com and download your free copy.

Don't forget

This software is free for you to use.

Click Download Now

Set up your new account in Web ceo

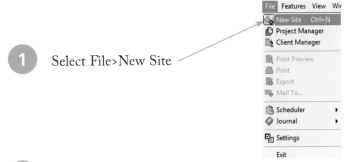

1 Select File>New Site

Don't forget

You will only need to add your details once as Web ceo will automatically remember them.

2 Enter your website details and description. Then click Next

...cont'd

3 Click Next

4 Double-check that all of the details you have entered are correct. Then click Finish

5 Congratulations, your new account has been created!

Now that you have successfully created your website account you will be able to use all of the tools that Web ceo offers.

This will save you valuable time as you do not have to enter your website details again.

3 Choosing your keywords

Keywords are the phrases for which you want Google to display your website. This chapter will explain how to choose and implement them.

Importance of keywords

The most important part of optimizing your website is the selection and implementation of your keywords.

If you do not get this part of the optimization process right then everything else you do will be in vain. Target the right keywords and your website will be a success; target the wrong keywords and you will miss out on the valuable traffic you are trying to canvass.

Keywords are very important to your website because without them your website theme will not be focused and as a result it is more likely that you will not rank well in Google.

Keywords should be identified and incorporated throughout the whole design of your website so that you can ensure it is focused on targeting the ones you have chosen. This will ensure not only that your content stays on track and is more relevant to your searchers but also that Google can see how relevant your website is. This will greatly increase your chances of gaining high positions within Google for search phrases that will generate real traffic.

Google can only recognize your site as being relevant to your desired keywords if you have used them in your website and in the links you have pointing to your website. This may sound very simple but most websites seem to miss out the keywords they are trying to target.

Some of the most common mistakes made when targeting keywords are:

- Targeting stop words
- Targeting keywords that are too broad
- Targeting too many keywords
- Targeting individual keywords
- Poorly representing keywords
- Not using different variations of keywords

Make sure that you do not make these common mistakes, as keyword selection is the foundation for your website's success within Google.

Don't forget

Keyword selection is the most important process in the optimization of your website. So it is worth spending time on it.

Using multiple keywords

Another common misconception in the selection of keywords is that when you are targeting keywords you should only identify and choose single words.

This is wrong and if you make this mistake you will almost certainly be disappointed with your results. To get top placements for single keywords (other than company names) is very difficult and will often take years to achieve.

The correct way to choose and target keywords is to select multiple keywords together in a search phrase. A search phrase is made up of several words that are very relevant and make a search more specific.

Optimizing with search phrases has many benefits compared to using single keywords, including:

- Less competition for your search phrase

- A more relevant website

- Better chances of a higher position in Google

For example, if we were to build a website to sell this book we would target the keywords "Google Book" and "Google Books", as this would be much more relevant for our website than just targeting the keyword "Book" – and we would have cut our competition down by a lot.

The other point to remember is that, although the broader keyword "Books" would get more traffic, it would not be as beneficial as you might expect it to be.

The simple reason is that if someone was interested in buying a "Google Book", that would be what they would search for, and through optimizing for that search phrase we would canvass the relevant traffic and not the irrelevant traffic.

The benefit of being specific is that we are only targeting relevant traffic. This is all we are interested in as this will more than likely convert into sales. The irrelevant traffic would probably only result in the selection of the Back button, which would be a wasted effort.

Hot tip

Using multiple keywords will dramatically cut your competition.

Don't forget

Keep your keywords focused to your website's theme.

Choosing your keywords

In order to choose your keywords you need to have a rough idea of the ones you think will be relevant.

First, put together a list of the keywords you would expect people to type into the search engines when looking for your product or services.

When you have your basic list of keywords it is time to bring in the reinforcements and put our new tools to work. It is always helpful to get a second opinion, and even a third, so we will use two different free keyword suggestion tools.

Web ceo keyword tool

Don't forget

Keep your keywords relevant and within your niche.

1 Select Features>Keywords

2 Select your website from the list

Hot tip

Don't just choose the keywords with the most traffic; look for keywords with low competition.

3 Click OK

4 Select the "Research keywords" tab. Enter your keyword phrase into the Keyword box and click Start

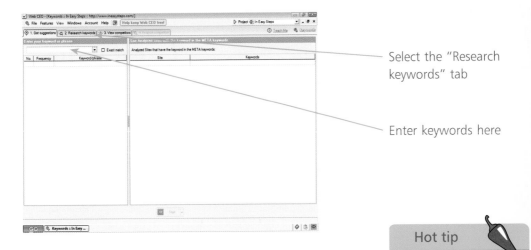

Select the "Research keywords" tab

Enter keywords here

5 Your search results will be displayed as shown:

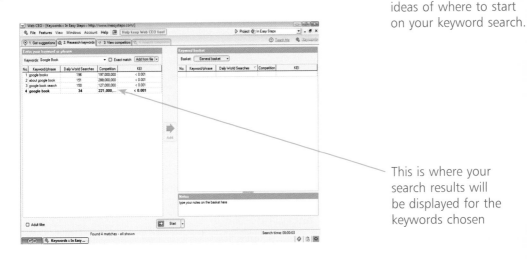

This is where your search results will be displayed for the keywords chosen

Hot tip

Use your competition's keywords to give you ideas of where to start on your keyword search.

Be sure to save your selected keywords to the basket so that you have them for future reference. You can always come back and add further keywords at a later stage as this should be a continuous process.

...cont'd

Yahoo keyword suggestion tool

To get started with this tool just follow the process below:

1 Type "yahoo keyword suggestion tool" into the Google search box and click Google Search

Google™

Web Images Video News Maps more »

yahoo keyword suggestion tool

Advanced Search
Preferences
Language Tools

Google Search   I'm Feeling Lucky

Advertising Programs - Business Solutions - About Google - **Go to Google UK**

2 Select the Keyword Selector Tool link

Keyword Selector **Tool**
Keyword Selector Tool. Not sure what search terms to bid on? Enter a term related to your site and we will show you:; Related searches that include your ...
inventory.overture.com/ - 2k - Cached - Similar pages

Resource Center: **Yahoo!** Search Marketing (formerly Overture)
Yahoo! Resource Center offering information and answering questions for your sponsored search ... **Keyword** Selector Tool · ROI Calculator · CPM Calculator ...
searchmarketing.**yahoo**.com/rc/srch/ - 8k - Cached - Similar pages

SEO Book **Keyword Suggestion Tool**
Is driven off the Overture **keyword suggestion tool**. Offers suggested monthly regional search volumes by market for Google, **Yahoo!**, and MSN. ...
tools.seobook.com/general/**keyword**/ - 13k - Cached - Similar pages

Overture (**Yahoo** Search Marketing) **Keywords** and Overture/**Yahoo** Bid ...
Lookup Overture (**Yahoo** Search Marketing) bid amounts and get Overture **keyword** suggestions on the same page with this FREE **tool** by Pixelfast.
www.pixelfast.com/overture/ - 2k - Cached - Similar pages

3 Type your keyword phrase into the box and click the blue arrow

Keyword Selector Tool

Not sure what search terms to bid on? Enter a term related to your site and we will show you:

• Related searches that include your term

• How many times that term was searched on last month

Get suggestions for: (may take up to 30 seconds)

Google book ◗

Note: All suggested search terms are subject to our standard editorial review process.

4 Your results will be generated as shown here. You can then evaluate these results to determine which keyword phrases will be most beneficial and relevant for your website.

Number of searches conducted for keyword phrase

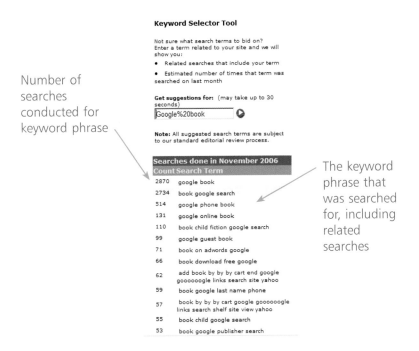

The keyword phrase that was searched for, including related searches

35

Now you have a new list of keywords. With the data you have collected from the two keyword suggestion tools, you are in a position to decide on the keywords to use.

The choice of what keywords to use is yours alone but you must carefully weigh up not only the number of searches the keywords receive but also how much competition there is for each of them.

Resist the temptation just to choose the keywords with the highest number of searches. Instead focus on search phrases that are related and in your niche as this will make top placements easier to achieve.

Don't copy, be unique

When you are trying to decide on what keywords to choose it can seem an easy option just to copy your competition.

This would be a big mistake as most of the time this is what your competitors have also done.

The worst part of it is that your competition may well be targeting the wrong keywords themselves, because they have not performed their own keyword research.

Too many people are just copying each other and taking it for granted that the keywords must be right because everyone else is using them.

The other problem that you will most likely find when you assess your competition's keywords is that they will be targeting lots of single keywords. This, as we know, is a big mistake and it will help you to identify the competitors that are not targeting effective keywords.

This is not to say that you should ignore what keywords your competition are using, as to do this could lead to you missing some good ones.

The knowledge gained from assessing your competition's keywords will help you get a better idea of the keywords you need to check and evaluate.

Some of these may prove to be relevant enough to use or they may even open the door to some new keywords you had not thought of using.

Copying your competitors' keywords without doing any other research, however, will cause you several problems including:

- More competition
- Unknown effectiveness of keywords
- Missing out on more effective keywords
- Lack of relevance to your website theme

Finding more unique keywords to target rather than just copying your competition will help your chances of gaining a higher position in Google.

Beware

Don't just copy your competitors' keywords, because if you do you will have no idea of what traffic you will receive and how relevant it will be.

Find your niche

The best and easiest way to top Google's listings, as we already know, is through having the most relevant site.

There is an easy way to help your website achieve this level of relevance. The way to be really effective is to find your niche and become the authority on it.

Many website owners try to optimize their websites for too many search phrases so that they simply spread themselves too thin and end up achieving none of them.

Most websites start off small with a limited number of pages. Instead of starting out with a small selection of finely tuned keywords, they try to rush in with every keyword they can think of and there is just not enough related content to make it effective.

For example, for "Google Book" all of our search phrases will be related to this search phrase. If we were to copy most website owners with our keyword selection we would be targeting all types of broad search phrases such as:

- Book

- Internet Book

- Search Engine Book

- SEO Book

We want to keep our website within a niche so we would be targeting keywords such as:

- Google Book

- Google Optimization Book

- Search Engine Optimization for Google

- Google SEO Book

Doing this will help keep our website theme very specific and Google will be in a much better position to see the true relevance of the site.

If we had followed the other method we would have diluted our website theme and we would not be deemed as relevant.

Hot tip

Creating a niche website will increase your relevance and make optimizing your site easier.

Don't use stop words

It is important when you are choosing keywords and search phrases that you do not use or include any stop words.

Stop words are words that Google considers to be irrelevant to its search results and so it ignores them.

These insignificant, frequently occurring words include:

Beware

Using stop words within your keywords will dilute their relevance.

- And
- A
- The
- In
- On
- Of
- Be
- I
- Me

Stop words will dilute the weighting of your keywords and search phrases and this is why it is important not to include them.

Google will ignore these stop words as it believes them not to be necessary in its process to asses the relevance of a website and finds that they just slow the process down unnecessarily.

This does not mean that you shouldn't include them in your website itself: you should. It would read very strangely if you did not include them.

You should use stop words in your body text but you should try to refrain from using them in your:

- Meta titles
- Meta keywords
- Links
- Header tags

4 Know your competition

Your online competition can hold the key to your success. Through careful analysis you can utilize their strengths and avoid their weaknesses.

Who are your competition?

One of the most important things when optimizing your website is to know your enemy.

Your competition hold the answers to how to get to the top of Google. You just need to know what to look for and how to analyze the data you find.

To know how to find your competition you must first have identified the keywords that you wish to target and found the sites that rank in the top results.

It is important to remember that your online competition are not normally the same competition that you have offline. Your online competition are the sites that appear in the top returned results for the search phrases you are competing for.

To identify your online competition, take your list of keywords and for each of them search Google. You should take note of the first 20 returned results and record these websites as they will be your online competition.

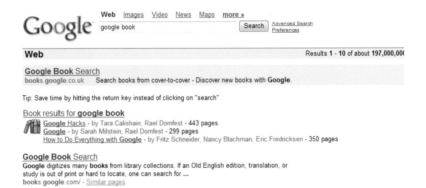

Once you have done this for your list of keywords it's time to analyze the results.

If you have got the keyword selection process correct you should find a correlation between the results: you'll see that the websites returned are normally very similar each time. You will usually find that one website will be in every set of returned results and this site is likely to be the most correctly optimized of the group and most relevant in Google's eyes. It is also likely to end up being your main online competitor.

Beware

Your online competition is not normally the same as your offline competition so avoid making the mistake of this assumption.

Hot tip

To find your main online competitor look for the site that is frequently in the top of the search results for the majority of your search phrases.

What keywords do they use?

Now you have identified who your competition are, it's time to look behind the scenes and see what keywords they are targeting.

To do this we are simply going to look at the HTML code of the website as Google would see it. This is perfectly fine to do and does not involve hacking into websites or any such illegal acts.

To look at the code just navigate to the required page, right-click on it as shown below and select "View Source". This will then open up a new page of text.

Hot tip

You can also view the source code by selecting Source from your browser's View toolbar.

Source code

```
<!DOCTYPE html PUBLIC "-//W3C//DTD XHTML 1.0 Strict//EN" "http://www.w3.org/TR/xhtml1/DTD/xhtml1-strict.dtd">
<html xmlns="http://www.w3.org/1999/xhtml" xml:lang="en">
<head>
<meta http-equiv="Content-Type" content="text/html; charset=iso-8859-1" />
<title>In Easy Steps: Homepage</title>
<meta name="Description" content="Computer Step is the leading computer books publisher,the world's favorite compu
<meta name="Keywords" content="computer books, internet books, in easy steps, computer book publisher,">
<link rel="stylesheet" type="text/css" href="./css/master.css" />
<!--[if lt IE 7]>
<link href="/css/iesucks.css" rel="stylesheet" type="text/css" media="screen" />
<![endif]-->
<!--[if IE 7]>
<link href="/css/ie7sucks.css" rel="stylesheet" type="text/css" media="screen" />
<![endif]--><script type="text/javascript" src="./js/scripts.js"></script>
<script src="http://www.google-analytics.com/urchin.js" type="text/javascript">
</script>
<script type="text/javascript">
_uacct = "UA-457659-6";
urchinTracker();
</script>
</head>

<body>
        <div class="skipper">
                <span style="display: none;"><a href="http://www.richardquickdesign.com">web Design Cornwall</a>.<
        </div>
        <div class="wrapper">
                <div class="top-nav">
                        <form id="search_form" method="post" action="./search/" onsubmit="return searchCheck('sear
                <div class="top-nav-search">
```

Don't forget

If your competition are only using single keywords, they are not making full use of their websites and are not correctly optimized.

Now that we can see the page as Google sees it, we can pick out the important Meta information to see what keywords they are targeting. We need to single out the three key areas of information that we are going to use to identify the keywords.

...cont'd

Meta tags

Meta Title

Meta Description

```
<html xmlns="http://www.w3.org/1999/xhtml" xml:lang="en">
<head>
<meta http-equiv="Content-Type" content="text/html; charset=iso-8859-1" />
<title>In Easy Steps: Homepage</title>
<Meta name="Description" content="Computer Step is the leading computer book
<Meta name="Keywords" content="computer books, internet books, in easy steps
<link rel="stylesheet" type="text/css" href="./css/master.css" />
<!--[if lt IE 7]>
<link href="/css/iesucks.css" rel="stylesheet" type="text/css" media="screen
<![endif]-->
<!--[if IE 7]>
```

Meta Keywords

Hot tip

Look for the keywords being used in all three of the Meta tags as these will be the ones your competition are targeting.

Beware

Do not assume your competition's keywords are correct and just copy them.

42

The Meta information is made up of three main parts:

● Title – This is displayed in the top of the browser to identify the page

● Keywords – The site would like to appear for when users search on these

● Description – This is the description of the webpage, to be displayed in the search results. (It is important to remember that Google does not use this description as it will create its own from the content of the page. Google still analyzes this tag and other search engines use it, so it should still be used.)

Don't forget

You can use your competition's keywords to help in your search for new keywords.

You should note the keywords used as you can assess these and decide whether you can or should be targeting them.

If the website is optimized, you will notice that some of the keywords will also appear in the description and title tags. These will be the main keywords they are targeting and you should note them down.

If you cannot find a correlation between the results of the different searches, it means that the websites are not optimized effectively and this will make things easier for you.

Who do they have links from?

Now we know what keywords your competition are targeting it is time to see who links to them. This may sound impossible to find out but with the Google toolbar it is made easy for you.

With your list of competitors' websites to hand, go to their home pages. Right-click on a page and navigate to Page Info; then select Backward Links.

This will then take you to Google, and waiting there will be a list of webpages that include a link to that page.

In Easy Steps: Linux in easy steps, 3rd edition
Linux in easy steps, 3rd edition. By Mike McGrath £10.99. Publication: December 30, 2005
Pages: 240 ISBN: 1-84078-305-2 ...
www.computerstep.com/books/details/?1840783052 - 25k - Cached - Similar pages

In Easy Steps: Tell a friend
Tell a friend. Fill in this form and submit it to your friend. You can edit the message text if you
wish. Your friend will then receive the information as ...
www.ineasysteps.com/site/tell/?1840782544 - 15k - Cached - Similar pages

In Easy Steps: eBay in easy steps - UK edition
eBay in easy steps - UK edition. By Nick Vandome £10.99. Publication: December 15, 2004
Pages: 192 ISBN: 1-84078-286-2 ...
www.ineasysteps.com/books/details/?1840782862 - 16k - Cached - Similar pages

You now know every web page that links to your competitors' websites and that Google rates. This information will prove priceless in the linking section. It will enable you to look to these sites to gain links into your own website, as you know they are interested in linking to sites like yours.

Hot tip

You can also check backward links by navigating to the home page and selecting the Backward Links option from the PageRank section of the Google toolbar.

Competitor positions

Your competition will be in the positions they are in for one main reason. Google believes their websites to be the most relevant for the search term queried.

Google will have arrived at this decision by running the websites through its algorithm. It will have found your online competition to be most relevant for those keywords, by analyzing and finding them and similar words in their:

Don't forget

You competition are in the place they are because Google has deemed that their websites are relevant to the specific keywords.

- Meta title
- Meta description
- Meta keywords
- Alt tags
- Header tags
- Main body of text
- Bold or highlighted areas
- Internal links
- External links

Google will also have looked at links on other people's web pages pointing to these websites, and analyzed the following points:

Hot tip

Use your competition to see how they have laid things out and used their keywords through the website to give you ideas.

- Quality of the site the link is on
- Link anchor text (text in the links pointing to the website)
- Relevance of the link (is it on a similar site?)
- PageRank of the page the link is on
- Number of other links on the page

All of these factors and more will contribute to your competition's search engine placements. It is through the analysis of this data that it is possible to find out why they are in the positions they are in.

Once you know what they have done, it makes it easier to create your action plan for achieving a higher position for your website.

How optimized are they?

To see what you need to achieve for your website, it is useful to see how well optimized a competitor's website is compared to yours. To do this, use Web ceo; add a new site but this time use your competitor's details, and then:

1 Select Optimize Pages

45

2 Select your competitor's website from the drop-down list provided and click OK

3 Select the Web page button. This will automatically update the box with the website details. Click Add Page

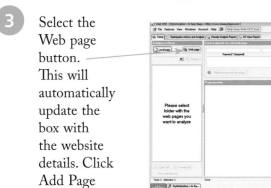

...cont'd

4 Select "Retrieve keywords from page"

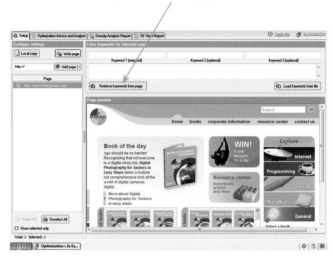

5 The results of the keyword search will be displayed in the
boxes at the top of the page

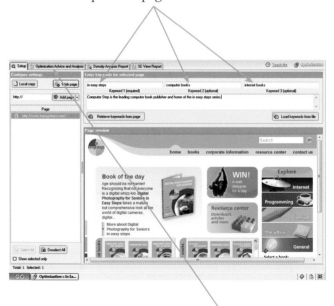

6 Select the Optimization Advice and Analysis tab

7 Select the Keywords you want to work with

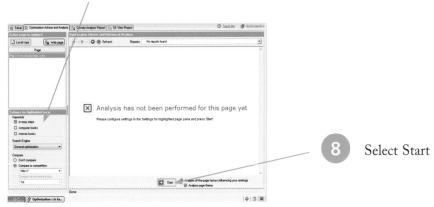

8 Select Start

9 Web ceo will then provide a summary detailing the problems with your competitor's website

Web ceo will produce a report analyzing your competitor's website. This report will show you what they are doing and what you are doing differently.

This report will enable you to spot the weaknesses in your competition and ensure your website does not suffer from the same problems as theirs.

How to top the competition

To top your competition and achieve a higher position in Google, you need to make Google see your website as more relevant than your competitors' sites.

This can sometimes seem like a monumental task but it can over time be achieved as long as you stick to Google's rules and work on increasing your relevance.

The first step is to analyze your competition and evaluate their websites to determine their strengths and weaknesses. Once you have done this it will help you to work out your plan of attack. You will be utilizing their strengths and learning from them. You will also need to learn from their mistakes and weaknesses and use these to give your website the upper hand.

There are three areas that you need to focus on for your optimization and these are crucial for gaining the edge over your competition:

Beware

If your competition are doing something that does not look right, do not just follow suit. Use the forums (see page 180) to make sure it is ethical.

- New relevant content creation – This is where you will create new content to help build the relevance of the site with Google and further help your website visitors

- On the page optimization – The optimization of your website. This is where you will make sure that it is targeted only to relevant keywords that will help to focus your chosen theme

- Off the page optimization – This is where you will work on increasing your inward links and securing a higher PageRank for your website than the competition have for theirs

If you concentrate on optimizing these three areas then you will be increasing the relevance of your website not just for your visitors but also for Google.

Over time, as Google re-crawls your website and sees it gaining in relevance as the new changes are introduced, Google's view on your website will become more positive.

This is the only way to achieve higher positions in Google's natural search. This, unfortunately, takes time to achieve but it is worth it in the long term. If you keep increasing the relevance of your website, you will keep increasing your position.

5 Setting up your website

The setting up of your website is one of the key parts of your optimization. If you get this part right, you will save yourself a tremendous amount of time and trouble in the future.

Domain name choice

The choice of your domain name can help with the optimization of your website as the name can be used to inform the search engines about the relevance of your site.

The first thing that your domain name will tell Google is what geographical area your website is targeting. For example, if you are using a .com name it is more likely that your site will be based in the USA whereas a .co.uk domain would be located in the UK.

This is not to say that you cannot use another domain extension. It is just easier to have your site identified correctly if you use the most appropriate extension for your country.

Example domain extensions and locations are:

- .com – US company

- .co.uk – UK company

- .net – US network

- .ca – Canadian website

- .de – German website

The second thing your domain can tell Google is how relevant your website is to your subject area. For example, if your site had the domain name www.google-books.com this would probably be because it was relevant to the content and so at a guess you would sell or have something to do with "Google books". Also as it is a .com it is likely that you are US-based.

It is important to remember that if you have a domain that is not relevant to what your website is about or your extension is not exactly what it should be, Google will tell in time but there can be confusion in the beginning until Google gathers enough information about your website to identify it correctly.

Don't forget

Use the domain extension that is relevant to your location.

Hot tip

Try to use your keywords in your domain name if possible to increase your relevance.

50

http://www.ineasysteps.com

Domain name

Extension

Hosting

The hosting of your website is a very important service and you should always do your research before you sign up. Google can use the location where your website is hosted to determine the country your website is targeting. This can sometimes cause unnecessary problems when you have hosted your website in a country other than the one you are located in and targeting.

For example, if you have a UK-based website for your UK-based company but you are using a .com domain extension and you are also hosting your website in the USA it could be very easy for Google to assume you are actually based in the USA.

This could prove difficult because you would not be shown in UK-specific searches (those that specifically target sites in the UK) and you would miss out on your most relevant traffic.

Normally when you are choosing your hosting, your decision will be based on cost alone. But there are many options you should consider before you sign up including:

- Cost

- Location of the servers

- Uptime of the servers

- Ease of contact with the provider

The uptime of your hosting provider is a very important factor that you should take into consideration when making your decision. Some service providers will now offer 100% uptime, which means that they will ensure your website is online and available 100% of the time.

This is a great benefit to you as the last thing you want when people choose to visit your website is to find they can not access it for technical reasons.

The other downside with this is that if Google tries to visit your website and it is not consistently available it cannot be confident that your site is reliable.

You may find that if your website is often down, Google may not rank it highly or may even remove it from the search results.

Hot tip

When choosing a hosting provider try to go on recommendations or ask relevant forums for advice.

Beware

Do not choose an unknown provider that you cannot contact easily just because it is the cheapest.

Validation and accessibility

The way in which your website is put together is a key factor in achieving higher positions in Google.

If your site's code is put together correctly this can help give you an advantage. It provides several benefits, including:

- Enabling Google to crawl your website more easily

- Reducing the risk of errors when the site is crawled

- Being more accessible to searchers and search engines

- Conforming to the W3C guidelines

Accessibility is an important issue on the internet and you need to make sure that you take this into account when you build your website or have one built. It is important to test your site to ensure that it has taken these things into consideration.

The W3C is an important committee that was set up to help with accessibility of web pages to all users on the internet. Since 1994 they have been publishing the standards and guidelines to help ensure the web reaches its true potential.

Tests for accessibility can be found on the World Wide Web Consortium website at www.w3.org. Depending on what technology your website has been built on, you will need to use the appropriate test.

If your website is validated, you may then insert the relevant logo on your website to display the fact that it does so. This is a good thing to display as it will show that you have taken these factors into consideration and that your website is accessible.

If your website fails to be validated, the testing tool will give you a list of reasons why, and you will then be able to rectify them and retest it.

Please note that for the example on the next page we will be using the HTML validator link as our website is in HTML, but you should substitute a different version for your website's technology if necessary.

To see if your web page validates, please follow the steps opposite:

Hot tip

If you are having a website built, always make sure it validates before you sign it off.

Beware

If your website does not validate you could be discriminating against people by not allowing them to access your material.

1 Navigate to www.w3.org

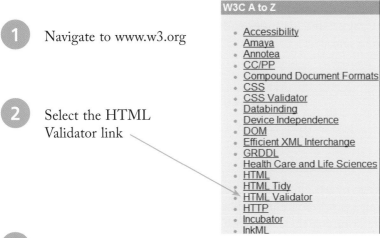

2 Select the HTML Validator link

Beware

Do not ignore errors found in the test. It is worth spending the time to correct them.

3 Enter your website address into the box and click Check

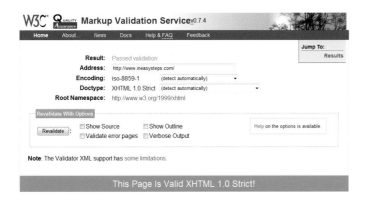

Validate Your Markup

Validate by URL

Address: www.ineasysteps.com [Check]

Enter the URL of the page you want to check. Advanced options are available from the Extended Interface.

Validate by File Upload

Local File: [Browse...] [Check]

Select the file you want to upload and check. Advanced options are available from the Extended File Upload Interface.

Note: file upload may not work with Internet Explorer on some versions of Windows XP Service Pack 2, see our information page on the W3C QA Website.

4 The validation details for your website will then be displayed as shown below

W3C Quality Assurance **Markup Validation Service** v0.7.4

| Home | About... | News | Docs | Help & FAQ | Feedback |

Jump To: Results

Result: Passed validation
Address: http://www.ineasysteps.com/
Encoding: iso-8859-1 (detect automatically)
Doctype: XHTML 1.0 Strict (detect automatically)
Root Namespace: http://www.w3.org/1999/xhtml

Revalidate With Options

[Revalidate] : ☐ Show Source ☐ Show Outline ☐ Validate error pages ☐ Verbose Output

Help on the options is available.

Note: The Validator XML support has some limitations.

This Page Is Valid XHTML 1.0 Strict!

Hot tip

You can also check your page by using the Validate by File Upload function before it goes live.

Page and file names

Page names are the names of the specific pages on your website. A page name identifies and separates that page from others on your site.

http://www.ineasysteps.com/books.htm

Page name

Hot tip

Use your keywords in page names and file names where relevant.

Page names should be used properly and optimized so that they can assist Google in deciding what your pages are about and determining their relevance. They will help Google to decide the relevance of each page both in terms of your website theme and of whether it should show the page in its results.

To optimize your page names and file names you simply need to know what keywords you are trying to target for each page and try to use them in the page names and file names where relevant. It is important to remember that you should not just cram keywords in; your purpose is to add relevance, not to mislead.

For our Google book website we would try to use relevant page and file names with our keywords included. So for our About page we would not use the name /aboutus.htm as this does not help increase our relevance or tell Google what the page is about.

Beware

Do not use your keywords excessively in each file name as this would be spamming.

We would instead use (depending on the keywords we had chosen for the page) /about-google-book.htm as this allows us to build in much more relevance.

Not only have we helped Google by telling it what the page is about, we have increased our relevance and helped optimize our page by including our keywords in the name.

This can be used for every page on the website and, if used properly, it can give you the edge over your competition.

You cannot use spaces in file names. If you wish to separate words you can do so by using – or _. This will ensure they are seen and interpreted by Google as separate words as it will see those characters as spaces.

It is very easy to change your page names if you have a static website but it can sometimes be more tricky if you have a dynamic website.

If you have a static website you simply need to edit the page name, which in most website publishing programs can be done by simply selecting the page and choosing the Edit option.

Most design packages, including Dreamweaver, will ask you whether you wish to automatically update your links, and for this you would select Yes.

This feature will ensure that all of your links that point to the old page name will now point to the new one. This is a particularly useful feature and will save you lots of time now and lots of problems in the future.

If you have a dynamic site you will need to contact your webmaster or the company that deals with your content management system to discuss whether it is possible to customize the page names.

Your webmaster may then be able to implement a facility that will enable you to name your own pages. Once this is implemented you will be able to edit your page names using your current content management system.

Next and most importantly you must put in place a 301 redirect, which will tell the search engines that the page has been renamed permanently and that they should update their records to reflect this. See the next page to learn how to do this.

If you have a new website that you are creating you do not need to worry about this, but if you are editing an existing website you must ensure you do it or you could end up with dead links and this will mean that traffic doesn't get to you.

Implementing a 301 redirect will ensure that any traffic going to the old page will now be redirected to the new page and ensure that your PageRank is transferred.

It is always worth getting your page names and file names correct at the creation of your website so that you do not have to worry about implementing 301 redirects later.

Hot tip

Dreamweaver will update your links automatically for you, saving you time and problems.

Redirects

Redirects are essential in the updating or changing of a website and must be used correctly. There are a few different types of redirect but we will only be concentrating on one type, the 301 redirect.

The 301 redirect is the most search-engine-friendly way to redirect traffic from one page to another. The 301 simply tells Google that you have moved a page permanently and where you have moved it to. This then enables Google to update its records and pass on any PageRank that may be attached to the page.

You should use a 301 redirect if you want to:

- Change a page's filename
- Move a page to another location on your website
- Move your whole website to another server

To implement a 301 redirect is very simple and easy to do. Here are the methods for the three most common technologies:

301 Redirect for pages using a .htaccess file on a Linux server

Open up your existing .htaccess file using Notepad. (If one is not available, create a Notepad page named .htaccess)

Insert the following line into the file:

```
redirect 301 /oldfolder/olddomain.htm
http://www.yourdomain.com/newfolder.htm
```

(To add more pages just duplicate this on new lines.)

Now change the relevant parts of the code to reflect your own website and page details.

Save the file and upload it to the root folder of your server, and you're done.

If you wanted to redirect a whole website you would just replace the line with:

```
redirect 301 / http://www.yourdomain.com/
```

Hot tip

Using a 301 redirect will make sure that Google knows your page has moved. It will pass on the PageRank to the new page.

301 Redirect for pages using asp (Windows Active Server Pages) on a Windows server

Delete all of the code from the old page and replace it with the following, substituting the names of your own domain and page.

```
<%@ Language=VBScript %>
<%

Response.Status="301 Moved Permanently"

Response.AddHeader "Location", "http://www.
yourwebsite.com/newpage.asp"

%>
```

301 Redirect for pages using asp.net (Windows Active Server Pages) on a Windows server

Delete all of the code from the old page and replace it with the following, substituting the names of your own domain and page.

```
<script runat="server">

private void Page_Load(object sender,
System.EventArgs e)

{

Response.Status = "301 Moved Permanently";

Response.AddHeader("Location","http://www.
yourwebsite.com/newpage.asp");

}

</script>
```

Once you have implemented your redirect you should navigate to the old page to make sure that it is redirecting correctly. This is imperative as you do not wish to lose traffic through dead links and missing pages.

You should also check whether you have any back links for the old page, and if so have the relevant sites update their records to point to the new page.

Beware

If you use the wrong redirect it will not work correctly.

Hot tip

If your required redirect is not given here, use Google to find it.

57

Cascading style sheets

Cascading style sheets, or CSS as they are more commonly known, are a very useful technology to take advantage of when creating your website.

Using CSS will give you many great benefits including:

● Complete control over the look of your website

● Site-wide changes by just editing one sheet

● Seperation of the design and the content of your site

The main benefit when it comes to using CSS on your website is that it allows you to keep its content separate from its structure. This makes for higher content weighting, which helps your site increase its relevance.

CSS is also very useful to Google as it does not have to go through everything and can just assess the content of your website, which is the part Google is interested in. Also, because you are keeping up with technology Google will view your website more favorably.

Using CSS can make the difference between Google having to go through this (a page without CSS):

Hot tip

CSS will help keep your keyword weight high.

Structure on page with content

...or this (with CSS implemented):

```
<div class="wrapper">
    <div class="top-nav">
        <form id="search_form" method="post" action="./search/" o
<div class="top-nav-search">
        <label for="search_box" class="hide">Search</label>
        <input type="text" name="search_string" id="search_box" value="Se
        <input type="image" src="./images/button_go.gif" alt="Go" />
        <input type="hidden" name="search_loc" value="ALL" />
        <input type="hidden" value="AND" name="search_type" />
</div>

        <div class="top-nav-lnks-holder">
            <ul class="link-list">
                <li><a href="./" class="lnk-wdth-1 on">hor
                <li><a href="./books/" class="lnk-wdth-2":
                <li><a href="./company/" class="lnk-wdth-:
                <li><a href="./resources/" class="lnk-wdt|
                <li><a href="./company/contact/" class="l
            </ul>
        </div>
    </div>
    <div class="breadcrumb">
        <h1 class="hide">Homepage</h1>
    </div>
    <div id="content">

        <div class="col-1">

            <div class="home-main-panel" style="background-im.
```

Content linked externally

Don't forget

Always check that your CSS validates to the W3C standards.

As you can see, using CSS is a very effective way of controlling the layout of your website.

You should also remember if you are using CSS to ensure that it validates by using the CSS Validator on the W3C website.

1 Select CSS Validator

2 Enter your website address into the box

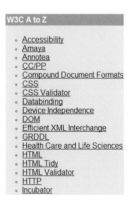

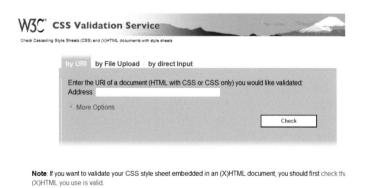

For more information on CSS and how you can make it work for you, see "CSS in easy steps".

Dynamic sites and pages

Dynamic websites are very common these days, especially for shops with a large number of products, and other sites with many pages of information. They can pose some problems with the optimization process but you can also turn this complex system around to work for you.

Dynamic websites use standard template pages that are populated from a database. This makes the information easier to store and manage.

The database structure can be a great help in your optimization campaign because, with some fine tuning, you can make it do some of the hard work for you.

For example, if you have a large database of products and you wish to optimize the Meta titles for their pages, and each Meta title needs to be the same as the product name, you could do this dynamically.

You could set up the database to input the product name into the page title for every page on your website. This alone could save you weeks and would mean you only needed to input this data once.

You could then use a similar rule for the Meta description tag, using the first line of the description of the product to populate the description Meta tag. This is one of the benefits of a good content management system.

If you are having a dynamic website built or are looking to buy an off-the-shelf package, be sure to ask the following questions to ensure the package will give you every chance of being able to optimize your website fully:

- Will I be able to choose and change my own page names?

- Will I be able to change the Meta information on each page?

- Will my pages validate and conform to the W3C rules?

- Will I be able to input Alt tags for my images?

- Will I be able to input heading tags?

Ensuring that your new dynamic site conforms to the above will save you time now and problems in the future.

Hot tip

Talk with your webmaster to see how your dynamic site can make the optimization of your website easier.

Beware

If you purchase a cheap content management system with no upgrade facility you will limit how much you can optimize your website.

Avoiding frames

It is very important to keep up with technology on the internet and keep your website current and moving with the times. This means avoiding using old and outdated technology that will work against your efforts to achieve a high placement in Google. It is therefore important to avoid using frame-based websites.

Using frames was a very popular option for creating websites in the early years. This has now become a very unpopular option as frames keep all of the details of your website off the page. This means that Google cannot see what we can see.

What we see:

What Google sees:

```
<html>
<head>
<!-- url = http://www.oscarenterprises.f2s.com/ -->
<meta http-equiv="Content-Type" content="text/html; charset=iso-8859-1"><tit
<frameset rows="100%,*" border="0" framespacing="0" frameborder="0">
<frame src="http://www.oscarenterprises.f2s.com/">
</frameset>
<noframes>
<body>
The website for britishbarbecue.co.uk can be found by clicking <a href="http
britishbarbecue.co.uk is registered through <a href="http://easily.co.uk">Ea
</noframes>
</html>
```

What we can see and what Google can see are very different and Google is unable to assess any of the content because it is hidden. This means that Google is totally reliant, when assessing websites that use frames, on the Meta information and inward links.

This is not a good situation to be in. If you have a website that uses frames it would be in your best interests to transfer it over to a newer technology.

Do's and don'ts

Setting up your website is a very crucial stage and should not be rushed.

Your website is going to be your online salesperson to the world and should properly and ethically represent your company.

This is why it is important that your website creates the right message.

If you put the effort into your website at this early stage and get it right it will pay dividends in the future and make optimizing your site easier and more effective.

When setting up your website, use the checklist below to ensure you are on the right track and not making silly mistakes:

When creating your website do:

- Use CSS
- Choose the right domain name and extension
- Ensure it validates before signing it off
- Host it in your own country
- Use redirects correctly
- Use a logical and optimized structure

When creating your website do not:

- Use old technology such as frames
- Go for the cheapest option
- Use non-customizable dynamic sites
- Rush and throw it together
- Hide text on the page with keywords in it

This is a very simple checklist but if you ensure you follow it you will be saving yourself time and avoiding major problems further down the line.

Beware

Do not accept second best from your web designer. Ensure you are happy before signing off the project.

Don't forget

Time spent now will ensure you do not have to redesign the site again in the near future.

6 Designing for Google

Searchers not search engines

When optimizing your website content, it is crucial to remember who will be reading it.

First and foremost you are writing your content for your human visitors.

Having a high position in Google is irrelevant if your copy does not read well. All of your efforts will be in vain because people will not be able to read and understand it.

This having being said, if you construct your pages properly you can easily satisfy both your human visitors and Google's search engine spiders. To do this you need to ensure that you do not get side-tracked with the creation of your content and you keep it specific and relevant.

It is easy just to litter and stuff your pages with keywords and hope for the best, but there are several problems with this approach:

- Google's algorithm can tell this is what you are doing

- Your copy will not read correctly

- Your website will not convert its searchers so well

- Your website will not be as relevant as it could be

The main problem is that even if this trick worked, when searchers got to your page they would not hang around for very long.

People don't expect to have to read through keyword-stuffed pages to find what they want. Searchers expect to find what they want in a logical, easy-to-digest order.

This makes the construction of your pages crucial so ensure you get the most from them by:

- Ensuring they are structured to inform on a personal level

- Ensuring the content talks of benefits to your readers

- Ensuring you use your keywords and other semantically similar words

- Using header tags where appropriate

Beware

If you forget about your human visitors when you create your content your efforts will be in vain.

Be unique

You should always ensure that your website's copy is unique and not duplicated anywhere else on the internet. This means that each of your own pages should be one of a kind, not exactly the same as others with a few words changed here and there.

Your web pages should all be relevant to your site's theme and you should use them to target different keywords. Each page is unique and you should target that page to canvass certain keywords. It is worth noting that not all of your visitors will enter your website through your home page. If one of your deeper, more specific pages is more relevant to the searcher's query, they will be taken directly to that page.

Google has a complex and sophisticated algorithm that is more than capable of spotting duplicated work. If it finds this, the pages will not be added to its database and they can be ignored. This would totally defeat the object of having created them in the first place. It is also worth noting that you should not in any case copy content from other websites and duplicate it without the website owners' written consent.

Google checks for duplication for several reasons including:

- Keeping search fast
- Keeping the results relevant
- Avoiding duplicated results
- Assisting to prevent copy theft

The main reason Google checks this is to ensure that its search results will always be relevant and delivered as fast as possible. After all, if we were to query Google with a search phrase and it delivered thousands of pages with exactly the same content it would be of little use to us.

There are times when your copy will need to be the same as that on another website if it is factual or a record of some sort. You can get around this by:

- Linking to the other page instead of copying the text
- Writing the page in your own words and laying it out differently

Beware

If you use text copied from another site on your page, Google will not add your page to its database.

Website theme

Every website should have a theme so that Google can tell what it is about.

The theme is determined by assessing all of the pages of the website to establish what they have in common.

This theme should always:

- Express the niche you have chosen for your website
- Include your main keywords

This is why it is so important to have a good structure, as it will make it easier to define your website theme.

To ensure your website theme is well defined you should ensure that your main keywords are included in:

- Meta title
- Meta description
- Meta keywords
- Alt tags
- Header tags

To make this effective, you should mix in your keywords with other relevant words for the individual pages. So for our Google book we would probably have something like the following page names:

- /google-book.htm
- /about-google-book.htm
- /google-optimization-book.htm
- /website-optimization-google.htm
- /google-seo.htm

This would ensure that our main keyword "Google Book" is seen as being very relevant to our website theme. By using other relevant words as well we not only make it more natural but we are also canvassing them as search terms, increasing our possibility of being found from other targeted search phrases.

Hot tip

A niche website theme will help you achieve better positions.

Don't forget

Ensure your keywords are linked into your website theme.

Content is king

When it comes to getting your website listed on Google, there is one thing that can make or break your chances more than anything else. Yes, you have guessed it: the content!

The content on your website is the main thing that will separate your site from all of the others on the internet.

Great content will:

- Increase your chances of Google finding you relevant and placing you in a good position

- Increase the likelihood of other websites in your industry linking to you

Content is what Google hungers for and it is always looking for new and more relevant content to show in its results.

If you have a website full of good content and you keep it up to date and add to it regularly, Google can tell. Google will then look to your website more often and visit it more frequently.

Every website in every industry can have good, useful and unique content. You can create useful content by creating:

- Relevant help pages

- Information pages

- Calculators

- Tips and cheats pages

- A relevant blog

- A free forum

It is this and this alone that will secure top placements, as this is what Google will derive the majority of its information on the page relevance from. Without content on your website you really have nothing to market and your website is of little use to your visitors.

If you have good and unique content you will start to find that people are linking to your website, which then helps your page optimization as well.

Beware

If you do not have relevant content, your website will never succeed in Google.

Hot tip

Ensure you know what keywords you want to target with your page before writing it, as this will help you use the keywords throughout your page.

Don't forget

Good, relevant content is what Google is looking for so ensure your site is where Google can find it.

Headers

Header tags are very important when it comes to optimizing your web pages and they need to be used sparingly, as their misuse or overuse will not work in your favor.

The six header tags

H1 — Header Tag 1 is the largest and therefore has the greatest value

Header Tag 6 is the smallest and therefore has the least value

The <h1> tag, as it marks the largest text, holds the most weight and importance with Google.

The <h6> tag marks the smallest headers and is considered the least important.

This is not to say that you should make all of your header tags <h1>, as that would look silly and also water down the importance of them all. The header tags should be used to help lay out your pages, with the main title being an <h1> tag and the next being <h2>, etc.

You should always try to use your main keywords for the page in your header tags along with the title and main content as this will increase the relevance.

Normally the header tags will appear at set sizes that may not fit in with your website's design but that is not a problem. You can set up a new cascading style sheet and set the sizes in that so that it will overrule the header tags' normal size, making the page look more normal.

Alt tags

Alt tags are the descriptions of the images used on your website.

These simple tags enable your website to be more accessible to all including Google. Alt tags are a necessity on every website that uses images for three main reasons:

- They make your site accessible
- They enable screen readers to interpret your images
- They enable Google to interpret your images

Many websites still do not use Alt tags correctly. They are not only breaking accessibility rules but are also limiting their positions in Google.

How we see images

How Google and screen readers see images

This is what the screen readers see when viewing the images

```
<a href="./resources/"><img src="./images/home/panel_re
alt="Resource center: Downloads articles and more" /></
```

Without use of the Alt tag, Google and the screen readers would have no idea what that image is about – and that does not help anyone. But if you populate the Alt tag with a relevant description this would enable them to tell what the image is.

If you do this everyone benefits including you because the more you describe your images, the more relevance you will build into your website – and Google will recognize this.

The other benefit is that more people can access and use your website so the chance of conversions increases.

Structure your page

Reasons to structure your website

- Keep things organized
- Help build your website theme
- Build in more relevance to your search strings
- Help Google crawl your website more effectively
- Make expanding your website easier

To add some structure to your website we would need to create some folders and move the pages to their relevant folders.

Remember to ensure that you update any links and set up redirects to the new pages to ensure you have no dead links. This will also ensure that the PageRank you have is passed onto the relevant new pages.

Content with no hierarchical order

- Index
- Who wrote the Google Book
- Who Published the Google Book
- How much is the Google Book
- Example of Google Book
- Ease of use
- Optimizing for Google
- Contact Google Book

Don't forget

Structure your website properly and you will make your life easier.

Note how all of the pages sit in one place with no hierarchical structure.

This means that you would be missing out on valuable opportunities to build in relevance to your website.

It would give each page a shorter URL as it would not include a possibly optimized folder name. As such, this would not create as much relevance as a structured one would.

Content in a hierarchical order

- Index
- About Google Book
    - ○ Who wrote the Google Book
    - ○ Who Published the Google Book
    - ○ How much is the Google Book
- How Google Book Works
    - ○ Example of Google Book
    - ○ Ease of use
    - ○ Optimizing for Google
- Contact Google Book

Note how all of the pages sit in their own relevant folders with hierarchical structure. There is an order present to help identify where each page sits.

The other benefit is the way the web address will be displayed to increase the relevance, and you can optimize the folder names to build in even more relevance. For example, instead of calling the services page folder of your website /services, why not be more specific? If you provide financial services why not call the folder that? This all helps Google see the relevance of your website and rank you accordingly.

Unstructured URL

http://www.ineasysteps.com/?9781840783322

Structured URL

http://www.ineasysteps.com/computer-books/
google-book.htm

The structured site has a longer URL for each page but it is more logical, it contains our keywords and it gives Google more information as to what the page is about.

Hot tip

Adding structure and more keywords to your search strings will add relevance to your website.

No optimized folder or page name included

Includes the optimized folder and page name

71

Meta tags

Meta tags are important things to get right on your website, as they will be telling Google what your site is about and helping it build an accurate website theme.

They will also be used to describe your website in the search results.

There are many different types of Meta tags but we will only be concentrating on the three main kinds:

- Meta title

- Meta description

- Meta keywords

This is how the three Meta tags look in the page source (please note that they should always be placed between the <HEAD> and </HEAD> tags).

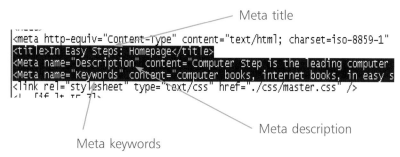
```
<meta http-equiv="Content-Type" content="text/html; charset=iso-8859-1">
<title>In Easy Steps: Homepage</title>
<Meta name="Description" content="Computer Step is the leading computer
<Meta name="Keywords" content="computer books, internet books, in easy s
<link rel="stylesheet" type="text/css" href="./css/master.css" />
```

The first and most important Meta tag is the Meta title tag, which is used and displayed at the top of the browser window and also in the title of Google's returned result for your page.

The second Meta tag is the Meta description tag, which is used and displayed in the description for your page in other search engine results. Google looks at this tag but it will display its own description, picked from your page, that is most relevant for the searcher's specific query.

The third Meta tag is the Meta keywords tag, which is where you can list the keywords that you feel would be relevant for your page. Google no longer places massive weighting on this tag as it has been so much abused, but it is still worth having as some of the other search engines will use it.

Hot tip

Ensure your Meta tags are individual and relevant to each page.

Beware

Ensure your Meta information is in the <HEAD></HEAD> section of your website source otherwise it will not be found.

Page titles

The page title is the most important tag that you will be using, as it is used to describe the page.

We talk about the title tag as being part of the Meta data when officially it is not, but for convenience we will include it with the Meta information.

Beware

Do not use the same title for every page.

Each page should have its own title that is not only unique and descriptive but also chosen to take into account the keywords for which you are optimizing the page.

The title tag will be displayed both in Google's natural listings in the search engine and also at the top of the browser window to identify the page.

Page titles in action

In Easy Steps: Homepage - Windows Internet Explorer

Title as displayed in browser

Title as displayed in Google search results

In Easy Steps: Homepage
Leading British publisher of computer books. Online shopping.
www.ineasysteps.com/ - 17k - Cached - Similar pages

The Meta title tag should always come directly after the opening <HEAD> tag so that it is found first.

To create the perfect title remember to:

- Include your main keywords

- Keep it page-specific

- Ensure it is in keeping with your website theme

- Keep it short and focused

Don't forget

Ensure the title tag is the first tag in your <HEAD> </HEAD> section.

Meta description

The second Meta tag is the Meta description tag.

The Meta description tag is used to describe your website to searchers looking at your site's result in the search engines.

Hot tip

Write your description as a pitch to get searchers to your website by using your keywords.

Google looks at this tag but it will display its own description, picked from your page. Google will display a snippet of your content that it believes to be most relevant for the searcher's query.

Although Google does not display this information, it will read and assess it and so it is still important to get it right.

In Easy Steps: Homepage
Leading British publisher of computer books. Online shopping.
www.ineasysteps.com/ - 17k - Cached - Similar pages

Description as displayed in Google

Meta description

```
<head>
<meta http-equiv="Content-Type" content="text/html; charset=iso-8859-1"
<title>In Easy Steps: Homepage</title>
<Meta name="Description" content="Computer Step is the leading computer
<Meta name="Keywords" content="computer books, internet books, in easy
<link rel="stylesheet" type="text/css" href="./css/master.css" />
<!--[if lt IE 7]>
<link href="/css/iesucks.css" rel="stylesheet" type="text/css" media="s
<![endif]-->
```

Don't forget

Write your Meta description for humans. Don't just separate keywords with commas.

Creating the perfect description

- Include your main keywords

- Keep it page-specific

- Ensure it is in keeping with your website theme

- Keep it short and focused

- Avoid repeating your keywords over and over

- Write it to be read not for use with the keywords tag

Meta keywords

The third Meta tag is the Meta keywords tag.

The Meta keywords tag allows you to input the keywords that you feel are most relevant to your page – the ones for which you wish your page to appear when Goole is queried.

```
<meta http-equiv="Content-Type" content="text/html; ch
<title>In Easy Steps: Homepage</title>
<Meta name="Description" content="Computer Step is the
<Meta name="Keywords" content="computer books, interne
<link rel="stylesheet" type="text/css" href="./css/mas
```

Meta keywords

Beware

You will not achieve high placements just by placing your keywords in the Meta keywords tag.

Google no longer places great weight on this tag as it has been so much abused in the past but it is still worth having.

This is because it is still likely that Google will look at the keywords here, and some of the other search engines will still use them.

This tag can also be useful for variations of words that you have not used. For example:

- Abbreviations of your keywords

- Semantically similar words

- Incorrectly spelt alternatives of your keywords

- Plurals of your keywords

It is very important to note that just because you put a word in your keywords, your page will not necessarily appear for that term.

If you have not mentioned the word in your content and you put it into the keywords tag, you are really just wasting your time.

Many people new to optimization believe this tag to be the be-all and end-all of optimizing a website, when really it is not.

Remember when using this tag to use search phrases, not just single words.

Hot tip

Use the keywords tag to target semantically similar and incorrectly spelt keywords.

Use your keywords

Use your keywords throughout your pages to ensure you get the most from them.

For some reason when people create a website they tend to forget to use their keywords. This is a big mistake because if you do not use them Google is not going to be able to see their relevance. This means that you are not going to appear in search results or rank well for them.

Your keywords should be used throughout your entire website, not just on one keyword-stuffed page. Each page on your website should have its own keywords that it targets. Each page should also be named appropriately to help target the keywords further.

Google uses something called "Latent Semantic Indexing", which is a technology within its algorithm. This technology examines the words on your website and can determine whether they are semantically close to each other.

When people write they will naturally use different words that mean the same thing; for example, the following words are semantically close:

- Search engine optimisation
- Search engine optimization
- SEO
- Organic SEO

Google would know that these words are similar and so they would add more relevance to your website.

If Google finds that your website is only using one keyword over and over again it can decide your site is unnatural-looking and you may not rank as highly as a result.

You should also consider this when building inward links as it will ensure that your links look more natural. It is always better to vary the anchor text in the links so that it looks more natural.

If Google believes that your website is gaining links naturally it will be looked upon more favorably and this will add more weight to your links and the keywords they use.

7 Optimizing your website

Optimizing your website is the key to ensuring that Google can see the true relevance of what you are offering.

How it was

In the early days, website promotion within the search engines was a much easier process than it is now.

The search engines used to rely purely on what the website owner said about the site. This meant that to optimize your website you only had to rely on your page optimization.

A website owner just needed to submit their site to the various search engines they wanted it to appear in.

The search engine would then send its spider to crawl the website and would store it in its cache so that it could be analyzed and then ranked.

The search engine would analyze a website based on the information the website owner had given in the Meta tags.

To optimize your website you simply needed to place the keywords for which you wanted to appear in the Meta tags, and that was about it.

People soon realized that if they gave a specific keyword in their Meta keywords tag more than a competitor did, they would appear higher than that competitor.

This meant that to appear at the top of the search engines for your keyword you had to have it in your Meta keywords tag more times than anyone else.

For example, if you put the keyword in your Meta keywords tag 10 times and your nearest competitor put it in 11 times, you would be second and they would be first.

To get into first position you would put it in your site 12 times. This spiralled out of control and caused the Meta keywords tag to have its value taken away. More complex algorithms were brought in to make the search results more relevant.

This way of assessing a website, based purely on the website owner telling the search engine what the site was about, was very much open to manipulation.

This offered no benefit to the searcher as the websites you were shown in your results could often have no real correlation with what you originally searched for.

How it is now

The way search was going, something had to change to ensure that it remained relevant.

Because of the abuse the Meta tags were receiving, the results that would be shown for your queried search could end up being totally irrelevant.

The search engines had to combat this, and they put in place more criteria against which to assess websites in order to determine their relevance. This was when the Meta keywords tag was given less importance, and less relevance weighting was placed on it.

The search engines started checking more points in their algorithms to ensure that websites were truly relevant, including:

- Meta tags
- Domain names
- Header tags
- Bold text
- Keyword weighting
- Keyword prominence
- Alt tags
- File names
- Link anchor text

A big change that was introduced was the use of off-the-page factors, which involved the analysis of what other sites said about your website.

Another big factor that has helped make search more relevant is Google's PageRank algorithm. This algorithm assesses the links that come into your website from others and judges how relevant and important those links are.

This has enabled Google to add a very important criterion when analyzing websites for relevance: how other people describe your website. This is a very useful tool, as other sites are less likely to be misleading and will give a truer representation of what your website is about than you would.

Hot tip

Utilize your inward link text to ensure that other sites increase your site's perceived relevance.

Don't optimize for your domain name

One common mistake often made by website owners is to optimize their sites for their domain names and/or site names.

This is a big mistake for several reasons:

- Your domain name is unique to you
- The site name will be represented throughout your site
- Your company name will be well represented naturally within your website
- You will dilute the other keywords you are using

The main way people misuse their domain names is to put them in every Meta title on every page before the keywords for which they are really trying to optimize, and this causes several problems including:

- Lowering the weight of your keywords
- Lowering the prominence of your keywords
- Detracting from your website's theme

In Easy Steps: Homepage - Windows Internet Explorer

Now by removing the domain name from the title tag and adding in some of your keywords, you will still rank for your domain name but you will increase the weighting and prominence of all of the other words in your title tag.

Computer Books - Windows Internet Explorer

The above title tag is now set up to help target our main keywords and will help with our optimization and the task of adding relevance to the website.

If you ensure that you do not optimize for your domain and company name you will make optimizing for your desired keywords much easier.

Analyzing your website

If you would like to assess your website pages and see how well optimized for Google they are, there is a simple way to check.

You can use the Optimization tool in the free software that you downloaded earlier from Web ceo.

This tool will assess the keywords you are using, and show how well represented they are within your website as a whole and on individual pages.

This will enable you to make sure that the keywords are well represented and that you stand a good chance of having a page that Google will find relevant.

You could analyze the page yourself but letting the software analyze it is by far an easier and more accurate option.

The software analyzes the top sites and works out what Google is looking for, based on the keyword representation throughout the site. It uses that to assess how close your website is to being the best.

How to analyze your website

1 Open Web ceo

2 Select Optimize Pages

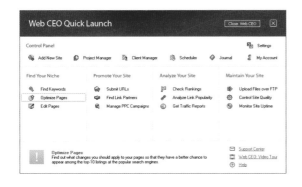

Hot tip

Ensure that you analyze new pages before putting them live on your website, in case you need to change them.

Don't forget

Web ceo automatically updates to ensure that its results are current.

...cont'd

③ Select the website you want to use from the drop-down list provided and click OK

④ Select the Webpage button. This will automatically update the box with your website details

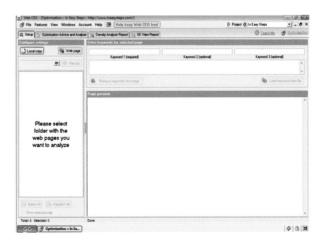

⑤ Select the Optimization and Advice tab

6 Check the keywords you wish to analyze and select "General optimization" from the left-hand column

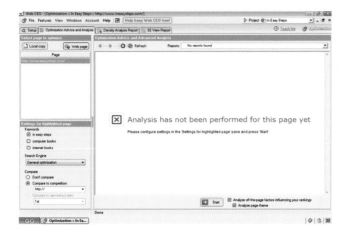

7 Click Start, and Web ceo will then automatically produce a detailed report on your website and how well optimized it is. This will be a general optimization report showing the details for your selected keywords

Optimizing your website

Now that you have analyzed your web page, the software will have generated a list of actions that you need to perform so that your page is optimized to meet the necessary criteria for your keywords.

It is important that your website is as close to this as you can get it, as it will then be in line with the top sites for your selected keywords.

Optimize your pages

 1 Take the first point on the report and investigate how you can bring your page in line with the report

2 Implement changes to your web page, ensuring that you are keeping true to your website's theme and that you avoid spamming (see page 85)

3 When you have done this, run the report again and check that the result is now in line with what is required

4 Move on to the next point and repeat the process

It is important to remember that you should never just stuff keywords here, there and everywhere, as it will not help you.

You should always ensure that your page stays true to what it is representing, and you will find by doing this that you are fairly well optimized.

Beware

Do not risk the content of your website by just inserting keywords to reach the limits suggested.

Hot tip

Try to ensure that your website is within the limits specified, to maximize your on-the-page optimization.

Spamming

Spamming is a big issue on the internet and you should ensure that you do what you can to avoid being responsible for spamming Google.

Spamming is when you deliberately try to mislead the search engines into including your web pages in their search results. This is done by using several different methods and tricks, including but not limited to:

- Creating keyword-stuffed pages to canvass traffic

- Excessive keyword repetition

- Hiding keywords on your page

- Using extremely small text

- Duplicated content

- Doorway pages (see page 184)

- Link farms (see page 185)

- Cloaking (see page 183)

- Keyword stacking (repeating the same keywords with variations in the case of the letters)

- Hidden links

- Typo spam (see page 186)

If you notice a website that it utilizing these or other spamming techniques you can report it to Google using the following link:

http://www.google.com/contact/spamreport.html

Benefits of reporting a spamming website to Google

Google will investigate a website that you report for spamming and may then:

- Remove the site from its listings

- Blacklist the domain

- Use the information to help make its algorithm better

Beware

Get caught spamming and you face having your site blacklisted and removed from Google's search results.

Do's and Don'ts

Optimizing your website is essential to enable it to be found on the internet.

If you follow the simple rules below you will ensure you have done what you can to optimize your website correctly. You will also avoid doing anything that could potentially harm your website's ranking within Google:

Do

● Ensure that you include your keywords in your Meta tags

● Ensure your file names and folders include your keywords

● Use a logical and optimized structure

● Use your keywords in your Alt tags

● Use your keywords throughout your content

Don't

● Keep repeating keywords in your Meta data or content

● Use misleading Meta data that is not related to your content

● Hide text on the page

● Have all pages in one folder

● Duplicate content

● Neglect to validate your pages

This is a very simple list but if you follow it you will avoid nasty penalties for spamming and misleading Google.

Dont risk Google's penalties

If you break the rules you could find:

● Your website blacklisted

● Your website sandboxed (see page 181)

● A reduction in your position

● Your website removed from Google's results

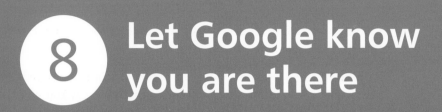

8 Let Google know you are there

Once you have your website set up and optimized it is time to let Google know that it's there.

Submitting your website

One way to let Google know your website exists is to submit it to the search engine yourself.

Submitting your website is a way of telling Google that it is there and asking Google to assess it for inclusion in its search results.

It is important to note that you need to submit your website to Google once and only once. It has been claimed that constant submission to the search engines will help your position in their search results, but this is not true.

Website submission is simply a way of telling the search engines that your site is there.

There are two ways that you can submit your website and they are both described in this section.

Submitting manually to Google

1 Go to the Google home page and click About Google

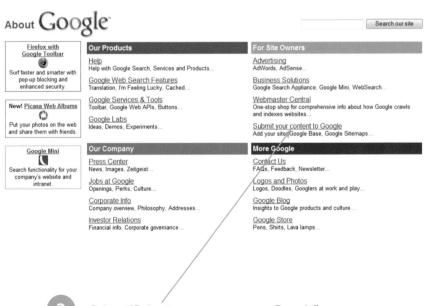

About **Google**

Search our site

Firefox with Google Toolbar	Our Products	For Site Owners
Surf faster and smarter with pop-up blocking and enhanced security.	Help Help with Google Search, Services and Products...	Advertising AdWords, AdSense...
	Google Web Search Features Translation, I'm Feeling Lucky, Cached...	Business Solutions Google Search Appliance, Google Mini, WebSearch...
New! Picasa Web Albums	Google Services & Tools Toolbar, Google Web APIs, Buttons...	Webmaster Central One-stop shop for comprehensive info about how Google crawls and indexes websites...
Put your photos on the web and share them with friends.	Google Labs Ideas, Demos, Experiments...	Submit your content to Google Add your site, Google Base, Google Sitemaps...
Google Mini	Our Company	More Google
Search functionality for your company's website and intranet.	Press Center News, Images, Zeitgeist...	Contact Us FAQs, Feedback, Newsletter...
	Jobs at Google Openings, Perks, Culture...	Logos and Photos Logos, Doodles, Googlers at work and play...
	Corporate Info Company overview, Philosophy, Addresses...	Google Blog Insights to Google products and culture...
	Investor Relations Financial info, Corporate governance...	Google Store Pens, Shirts, Lava lamps...

2 Select "Submit your content to Google"

3 Click "Add your URL to Google's index"

How to submit your content to Google

 Add your URL to Google's index
We add and update new websites to our index every time we crawl the web; we invite you to submit your top-level URL to make sure we don't miss your site.

 Google Base - New!
Google Base is a place to which you can easily submit all types of online and offline content, which we'll host and make searchable online.

Google Webmaster Tools
Google's suite of webmaster tools provides you with a free and easy way to help improve your site's visiblity in our search results.

Beware

Over-submission of your website may have a negative effect on your results so submit it only once.

4 Enter your URL (your website's address) and the security code that appears in the box, and then click Add URL

Add your URL to Google

Share your place on the net with us.

We add and update new sites to our index each time we crawl the web, and we invite you to submit your URL here. We do not add all submitted URLs to our index, and we cannot make any predictions or guarantees about when or if they will appear.

Please enter your full URL, including the `http://` prefix. For example: `http://www.google.com/`. You may also add comments or keywords that describe the content of your page. These are used only for our information and do not affect how your page is indexed or used by Google.

Please note: Only the top-level page from a host is necessary; you do not need to submit each individual page. Our crawler, Googlebot, will be able to find the rest. Google updates its index on a regular basis, so updated or outdated link submissions are not necessary. Dead links will 'fade out' of our index on our next crawl when we update our entire index.

URL:

Comments:

Optional: To help us distinguish between sites submitted by individuals and those automatically entered by software robots, please type the squiggly letters shown here into the box below.

Don't forget

Google will find your website through its links so submission is only a precaution.

5 Your URL will now have been successfully added to Google's crawl list

...cont'd

Submitting your website using Web ceo

1 Open Web ceo and click Submit URLs

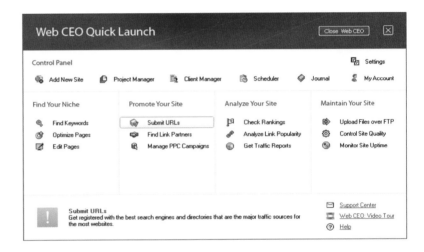

Hot tip

By using the submission function on Web ceo you can submit to all of the search engines at the same time.

2 Select the website you wish to add from the list or select New Site

3 Click "Populate from Main page" to fill in the required fields

4 Enter other details manually and click Save

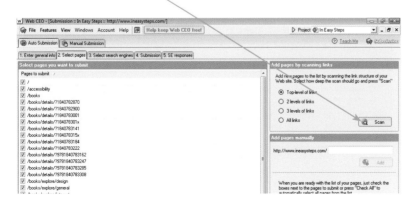

5 Select the "Select pages" tab and automatically update the pages you want to submit from your website by clicking Scan

...cont'd

6 Select the "search engines" tab and then click "Search engines list" to automatically produce a list of search engines to which you can submit your website

Select the relevant search engines by location or language.

7 To select search engines by country select Check>Check by Country>Other countries and then select the country that is most applicable to your website

8 Now set the rules for your search engine submission and click "Set default submission rules"

9 Select the Submission tab

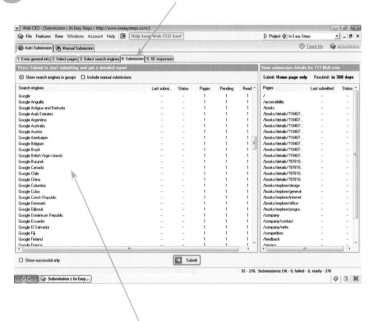

10 A list of your selected search engines will then be displayed along with the website pages you have selected to submit. You can manually select the pages you want to include for each specific search engine or by pressing Submit you can automatically include all the pages of your website that you chose at the beginning

11 By selecting the "SE responses" tab you can see a report showing which submissions have been successful

Linking into Google

One sure way to get into Google's listings and make sure it knows you are there is via linking.

If you have just one link into your website from another site that is crawled by Google, then Google will find you without you having to do a thing.

You only need to get one link on a regularly crawled website for Google to find your website.

If you have no links into your website there is no connection, and the only way Google will know that you are there will be for you to tell it by submitting your website. This process could take a long time if Google has many sites already in its queue waiting to be crawled.

Having links pointing at your website is a much easier and faster way to have your site crawled.

Google finds your website through other links by sending its spider out to crawl the internet. The spider will find out the current results so that it can update its search results so that they stay up-to-date and relevant.

If you have a link from one of the websites crawled then the Google bot (the spider) will find your site through that link.

Google will then index your website and consider showing it within its search results for search phrases for which it considers your site to be relevant.

The extra benefit with this method is that through creating links into your website you will also be helping to optimize your off-the-page factors (see page 185). If you have optimized inward links then you are also increasing your website's relevance and the chance of a good position for your optimized keywords. See the next chapter for more information about this.

This will all work together to get Google to notice your website and will give your site the opportunity to be included in its search results.

Optimized inward links will also help increase your PageRank, which is another major factor that Google uses when assessing the relevance of websites for keywords.

Creating your sitemap

Once you have your Google account activated (see page 22), you just need to create your sitemap and upload it.

1 Navigate to www.sitemapspal.com and enter your domain name in the box

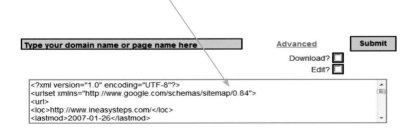

2 Check the Download box and click Submit

3 The information in the red box needs to be downloaded and saved as a new text file named sitemap.xml

| Type your domain name or page name here | Advanced | Submit |

Download?
Edit?

```
<?xml version="1.0" encoding="UTF-8"?>
<urlset xmlns="http://www.google.com/schemas/sitemap/0.84">
<url>
<loc>http://www.ineasysteps.com/</loc>
<lastmod>2007-01-26</lastmod>
```

4 This sitemap.xml file must now be uploaded to the root folder of your website on your server so that the next step of submitting to Google is possible

Google sitemap submission

Now you have created your sitemap you need to log into your Google account and let Google know it is there.

To sign up to Google sitemaps and upload your sitemap follow the steps below. (Ensure that you have uploaded your sitemap to your webserver root folder as /sitemap.xml before you start this process.)

1 Sign in to your Google account. Select the Webmaster Tools link and type your website address into the box. Then select OK

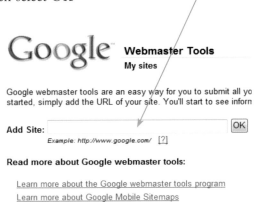

2 Select the Sitemaps tab. Then click Add a Sitemap

3 Now select the type of sitemap you wish to apply, normally General Web Sitemap

Add Sitemap

You can add a Sitemap to your account Sitemaps tab. [?]

Add General Web Sitemap ▼

Choose type...
Add General Web Sitemap
Add Mobile Sitemap

4 Enter the URL of your sitemap into the box and click Add Web Sitemap

1. I've created a Sitemap in a supported format. [?]

2. I've uploaded my Sitemap to the highest-level directory to which I have access.

3. My Sitemap URL is:

Example: http://www.ineasysteps.com/sitemap.xml

Add Web Sitemap

Don't forget

You need to upload your sitemap to your web server for Google to find it.

5 Google will now confirm that it has queued your website to be crawled

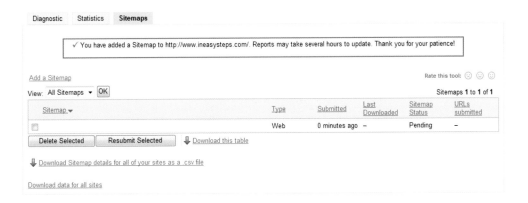

| Diagnostic | Statistics | **Sitemaps** |

✓ You have added a Sitemap to http://www.ineasysteps.com/. Reports may take several hours to update. Thank you for your patience!

Add a Sitemap

Rate this tool: ☹ ☺ ☺

View: All Sitemaps ▾ OK

Sitemaps **1** to **1** of **1**

Sitemap ▾	Type	Submitted	Last Downloaded	Sitemap Status	URLs submitted
☐	Web	0 minutes ago	–	Pending	–

| Delete Selected | Resubmit Selected | ⬇ Download this table |

⬇ Download Sitemap details for all of your sites as a .csv file

Download data for all sites

Google will have added your sitemap to its crawl list and will soon visit your website and start feeding back information.

It is a good idea to check back after one to two days to ensure that your Google sitemap has indeed been crawled and that there have been no problems with the process.

Occasionally you will find that there has been an error while crawling your sitemap and you may need to repeat the process. Google will report back if it experiences a problem and detail what the error entailed, so you can correct it.

Keeping it up to date

It is very important that when you have created your Google sitemap you keep it up to date.

This sitemap will enable you to inform Google every time you make a change to your website.

To update your sitemap you just need to:

1 Navigate back to www.sitemapspal.com and recreate your sitemap

2 Upload your new sitemap to your web server (see pae 95)

3 Login to your Google sitemap account and upload your new sitemap

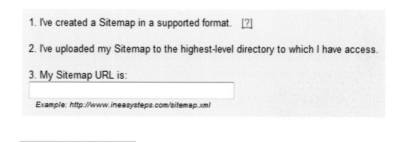

Every time you update your website this process must be repeated to ensure that your Google sitemap accurately reflects your website's content.

9 Linking to your success

One of the most effective ways to achieve great results with Google is to create links to your website. These links are important, but even more so are the sites they are from and the text in the links. In this chapter you will learn about the links you need and the links to avoid.

Why links are important

Hot tip

Good inward links will greatly increase your chances of good positioning.

In Google's mission to make search more relevant it will utilize all the information it can find about your website. This includes the information it finds in your incoming links.

Inward links help Google determine:

● What your website is about

● What keywords are relevant to your site

● How important your site is

● Where your site is located

Google will utilize this information to assess where it should place your website in its results. This place will of course depend on how relevant your website is deemed to be for the particular search term queried.

Google gives great weight to what other websites are saying about your site. This has proved to make search more relevant and the results displayed more helpful to the searcher.

This is because other websites are more likely to be impartial and truthful about your website and what it is about than you would be.

This is why when you evaluate a website you can find that it ranks very highly for a search term never really mentioned in it. If you then check the back links for such a website you will most likely find that it has many relevant sites linking to it using the specific keywords as the link anchor text.

Google relies on what other websites are saying about your website for your off-the-page optimization. This includes:

● What anchor text is used

● The theme of the website the link is on

● The theme of the page the link is on

● The PageRank of the website the link is on

PageRank

To evaluate web pages properly, Google uses its PageRank algorithm.

This complex algorithm is used to determine how important web pages are, based on the links they have coming into them, and of course the value of those links.

PageRank displayed in the Google toolbar

To see the PageRank of a web page, hover the cursor over the green bar in the Google toolbar

Google counts each link into your website as a vote from that website for yours, and likewise if you link to another site, that would be counted as a vote for that site. This is a very simple explanation as the algorithm will take into account much more that just the number of links you have coming into your website.

Google also takes into account many other factors, including but not limited to:

101

- Quantity of links

- Relevance of each link

- Text in the links

- The PageRank of the sites you have got the links from

- The importance of the sites you received the links from

- Whether the links are one-way or reciprocated

Important websites have a higher PageRank. If you get one relevant link from an important site, it will mean more than a thousand non-relevant links.

Google uses sophisticated text-matching techniques to ensure that it knows just how relevant your links are. These techniques tell it what every website, including yours is about. If your links come from websites that match yours, this is of greater importance than if there is no relevance involved.

Types of link

There are three types of link that we are going to be concentrating on. At some point you will need to use all of them.

The inward link

This is the most important type of link when it comes to optimizing your website as it will really help you increase your site's relevance and PageRank. An inward link is simply one that someone else creates from their website to yours. You do not have to link back to their site.

The external link

This link can be used to help build relevance for your website by linking it to other relevant sites. This is useful if it will help the people who are visiting your website.

The reciprocal link

This type of link is normally used as a trade where one site will link to another on the condition that they link back. This can still be useful but only if the website is relevant to yours and will be of value to your website visitors.

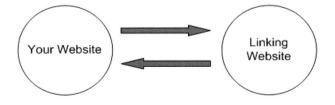

Spamming

Spamming is a serious problem on the internet. You must always be aware of what you are doing and ensure that your activities are not spamming in any way.

Spamming can have serious effects on your website including:

- Giving it a bad name
- Associating you with bad websites
- Giving your company a bad name
- Losing your relevance
- Making you very unpopular

Link building can sometimes seem a very tiring task and it can often seem tempting to use one of the many automated alternatives available on the web.

This is not a good option as they actually just spam your link to various places that do not want it and will just remove it, including:

- Blogs
- Forums
- Guestbooks
- Directories
- Contact forms
- Feedback forms

If you use these methods you will end up, at the very least, getting your company and website a bad name, as people hate spam and therefore hate the people who use it.

The other problem with using this software is that you have no real knowledge of what sites your links could appear on and how you will be linked to. The last thing you want is to have your link appearing in bad neighborhoods as this could seriously harm your website and even your company.

Beware

Spamming people's websites is a fast way to get your site a bad name.

Hot tip

Stay away from automated link-building software as it will rarely benefit your site.

Beware

Do not link out to websites that are spamming or you can be penalized.

Internal linking

Internal links are the links that you use within your own website to link your pages together, enabling searchers to navigate around your site.

There are two different types of internal link that you can use to navigate around your website:

Absolute links

Absolute links use the whole URL including the domain name and extension.

```
<h2 class="swit
<div class="hom
    <a href
a href="http://www.ineasysteps.com/books/details/?1840783184">
a href="./books/details/?1840783222"><img src="./images/books/
a href="./books/details/?1840782870"><img src="./images/books/
a href="./books/details/?1840783001"><img src="./images/books/
a href="./books/details/?9781840783247"><img src="./images/boo
```

Relative links

Relative links use addresses that are relative to where the link is placed on your website. They are the most commonly used.

```
a href="./books/details/?1840783184"><img src=".
a href="./books/details/?1840783222"><img src=".
a href="./books/details/?1840782870"><img src=".
a href="./books/details/?1840783001"><img src=".
```

One thing often overlooked when websites are designed is the detail of the links used to navigate around them, or more importantly the text in those links. This text is called anchor text and it contains the hyperlink that takes you to the other page on the site.

The text "site map" is the anchor text in this example and if clicked it will take you to the sitemap page.

You can really help add to the strength of your website theme by making use of the anchor text in your internal links.

Most internal links will have "click here" as the anchor text but this is pointless and adds no relevance to your website whatsoever. Instead of using "click here" as the anchor text you should be using the relevant keywords for that page, as this will add relevance and help Google to see what the page is about.

If, for example, the page you are linking to is the one that you have optimized for the search phrase "Google Book", then make sure that the internal links you are using to link to that page make use of that keyword.

You do not always have to use the link text "Google Book"; remember you can use semantically similar words and words that will be relevant to that page including:

- Google Books

- Book on Google

- Optimizing your website for Google

- Google SEO

- Getting your website found on Google

- SEO for Google

Beware

Ensure that you only use relevant keywords to link your pages together.

The other great thing about mixing your anchor text up is that it will not only look more natural but it will also stand a higher chance of ranking under a mixture of all of the keywords used.

Optimizing your link anchor text is easy to do and helps build relevance for your website and the pages that the links refer to.

By using optimized link anchor text instead of irrelevant text such as "click here" you will be:

- Optimizing your website for your keywords

- Helping your website visitors navigate easily

- Helping Google tell what your pages are about

- Strengthening your website theme

Finding links

Most people struggle when finding places to get links from but it is actually relatively simple. Below are some common ways to find links:

Ask Google

One easy way to find links is to ask Google. To do this follow the steps below:

1 Open up Google

2 Do a search for your desired keywords

3 Navigate to the top sites to see whether they allow you to submit a link

Alternative option

1 Open up Google

2 Search for your niche (for us it would be "Google Book") and include "+ links, + link, +site" at the end of your keywords. Google will look for sites that contain references to each

3 Then just submit your link to the relevant sites

Finding links in Web ceo

1 Load Web ceo and select Find Link Partners

Promote Your Site

    Submit URLs

    Find Link Partners

    Manage PPC Campaigns

2 Select the website from the list provided or select New Site. Then click OK

3 Click Configure

4 Select which search engines you wish to check for links. Then click OK

5 Select the "Add keywords" tab. Then select Add. To download keywords used in your website click "Get keywords from site"

6 Your website will appear in the screen; then click OK twice

7 Click Find New Partners and a list of potential linking partners will now be produced

How to request links

Once you have identified the places you would like to get links from you need to find a way of requesting them.

There are two ways of doing this depending on the way they want you to apply for a link.

The form

Spend some time on each of the forms so that your details read correctly, as badly filled in forms will not be accepted.

The first and most common option is that they have a standard form on their website for you to fill in and request a link

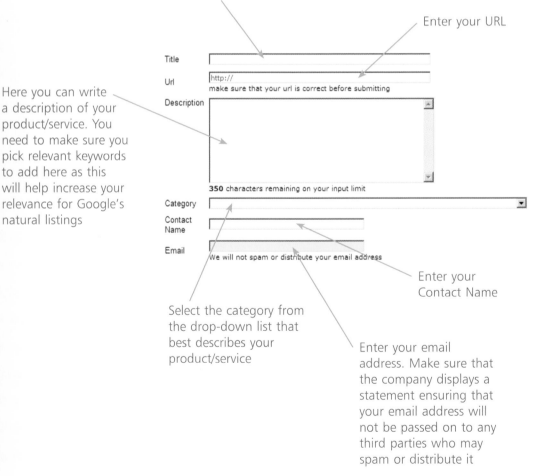

Enter a specific title relating to your product/service and remember to include your relevant keywords

Enter your URL

Here you can write a description of your product/service. You need to make sure you pick relevant keywords to add here as this will help increase your relevance for Google's natural listings

Select the category from the drop-down list that best describes your product/service

Enter your Contact Name

Enter your email address. Make sure that the company displays a statement ensuring that your email address will not be passed on to any third parties who may spam or distribute it

The email

The second method is when the site owners ask you to email them (sometimes they won't have asked you but you will see that your site can add value to their visitors).

It is very important that when you send an email requesting a link for your website you take the time to construct it properly. If you do not spend time on the email to make it personal and get your message across, the likelihood is your email will go directly into their deleted items folder.

There is lots of automated software out there that can just select a long list of websites and send the same generic email to them all. On the face of this it sounds tempting as it doesn't take very long but the actual links you will get out of it will not be many.

To really make the most of your linking you need to send a personal email to the owner of the site or the person named on it as the email contact, remembering the following:

- Try to use their name – it looks more personal and less automated

- Introduce yourself, your website and your company

- Compliment them on their website and say which bits you liked

- Tell them why they should link to your website

- Explain the benefits of linking to you for them and their visitors

- Tell them where you have placed their link, if applicable

- Suggest how they should link to your site, what page you would like your link to be on, what page to link to and the text to use

- Thank them for their time

- Sign it from yourself

Remember that when requesting links you need to be personal and properly explain why they should link to you to get the most from this.

Hot tip

Personalized emails will get a more positive response.

Resource page

If you are going to be linking to other people's websites the chances are you are going to need to reciprocate some of the links.

You will therefore need a page on which to place the links that you will reciprocate.

To set up this page you will need to create a new page using your website design package and name it appropriately.

Don't forget

You only want to accept relevant links into your resource page to help build your website theme.

For our "Google Book" website we would name our page something like:

- /google-book-resources
- /google-seo-resources
- /google-optimization-resources
- /google-book-links
- /google-seo-links
- /google-optimization-links

Once you have created this page you should put some text on it to describe the page. This should inform visitors that this is a page of resources that you feel they will find useful and relevant.

You should also include instructions on how people could add their links to this page. This could be a simple message explaining: "To appear here please link to our website using one of the following links". You will of course need to mention that their website should be relevant to your subject or it will not be included.

You would then create several different links that they could choose from, all with relevant and optimized anchor text to help your website gain relevance.

You can give your visitors two ways of submitting their links to you, by either:

- Using a form, or
- Emailing you their links

Let the links come to you

One of the most effective ways to get incoming links is by letting them come to you.

If you have created a good website with good, unique and relevant content then people will naturally want to link to you to enhance the value to their visitors.

Attracting links in this way has now become known as link baiting and although it sounds bad it is actually a really good and useful way of attracting links to your website. You can better equip your site to do this in several different ways:

- Offer something unique that can only be found on your website

- Give something away, such as a report or a document

- Have a unique online tool

- Coin a new saying or phrase in your industry and get people talking about it

- Give away a tool that others can use on their websites but only by linking back to you

- Have a game or quiz

- Be the first to document something

- Upload a useful film or documentary

- Become an expert in your niche and write about it

There are many different ways of doing this but you will need to find one that sits well within your website and industry.

Doing this will not only increase your inward links but you will find that:

- The links are from places to which you could not just submit your site

- The links will look more natural

- The anchor text will be varied, enabling your website to rank for more keywords

- Your website's relevance will increase

Hot tip

Link baiting will save you time as you will gain links naturally.

Links you need

There are links you need and links you don't. Get the right links and this will help your website achieve higher positions in Google. Get the wrong links and your efforts will be wasted.

Links you need

- Are from well-known websites

- Are from sites with a high PageRank

- Are from sites with few links on the page

- Are from sites that have relevant optimized anchor text

- Are from sites with a relevant theme

- Are static with a normal hyperlink

Links you do not need

- Are from non-relevant pages

- Are from unethical websites that use spam

- Are with hundreds of non-related links on the page

- Are hidden from the searchers' view

To see how important a website is to Google we can use the PageRank bar in the Google toolbar to help us decide.

Don't forget

You must only work to gain links from relevant websites.

You should look at the PageRank for not only the home page but also the page where your link would be placed. If the page is full of links it will not be worth as much to you, as the PageRank will be split between all of the links on that page.

Also you should always try to get inward links for which you do not have to give a reciprocal link, as they will be more valuable than reciprocated links.

Get the most from your links

To get the most from your links you need to make sure you do the following:

- Get the links from pages with a good PageRank

- Make sure the sites are relevant to yours

- Vary the keywords that you use in the anchor text

- Vary the descriptions in your link

You must select the right place to put your links in order to get the most relevance from them, and ensure the website has a good PageRank:

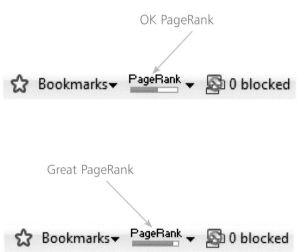

The higher the PageRank of the page, the more valuable a link on that site would be. You need to remember that the number of links on a page will influence how much of the vote you get; fewer links mean you will get more of the vote.

The main thing you must do is vary the keywords you use as your anchor text. This is important as it will look more natural, and because it looks more natural you will most likely achieve higher positions. Google knows which words are similar and by using similar keywords you will be optimizing for all of them at the same time.

Directory linking

Directory linking is a great way to source links for your website.

A directory is simply a website that houses links to other sites and places them in an organized order. This makes it easier for people to find what they are looking for. There are thousands of directories out there, from the general directories to the niche directories.

Some directories are free and with others, like the Yahoo directory, you have to pay to be included. This being said, most of the directories charge only a few dollars to submit your link.

You can use directories to gain many useful links from relevant categories and in most directories you can even choose your own anchor text and descriptions.

To find directories to submit to for your industry, you can simply ask Google again.

To do this follow the steps below:

1. Navigate to the Google search box. Following on with the keyword that we have been using as an example you would type "directory+google book" into the search box and click Search

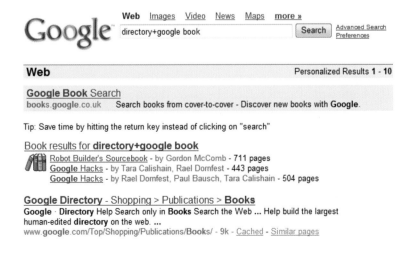

This will then return a list of directories from which it could be useful to get links.

There is also a handy list that has been created, with many of the directories in it and information on each of them. The directory list is also split into sections for different industries to make it easier to navigate, and it can be downloaded as a free Excel spreadsheet.

1 Navigate to http://info.vilesilencer.com

2 Click the Excel Download link

3 Click Save to save the list to your computer so that you can refer back to it at a later date

Don't forget

Spend the time to submit to the directories properly otherwise they will just delete your application, as they do not have time to fill in the gaps.

The great benefit with directory linking is that most of them do not require a reciprocal link, so this is a great way of building quality, inward non-reciprocal links to your website.

Another great benefit with directory linking is that because directories take different amounts of time to assess and add your link to their listings, you will end up with a steady, gradual stream of new links, which will look more natural to the search engines.

Effective articles

Writing articles is also a very good way to gain inward links into your website. The way to do this is by writing articles on your niche subject. This will help you not only to generate a good number of inward links to your website but to establish yourself as an authority in your field.

Writing your Articles

If you write your article as sales copy people will tend not to use it.

When you write an article it can be on any subject as long as it will be relevant to your website. After all, if it is not relevant you will struggle to get it on the websites that will give you the best links. It is important to remember when writing your article to:

- Make it relevant to your niche

- Keep on track and structure it well

- Ensure that the article will benefit the readers

- Avoid plugging your own website or business in the text

Getting your articles noticed

Once you have written your article you will need to distribute it and you can do this in several different ways:

- Submit your article to related niche websites

- Use article submission software

You can seek out and submit your article to niche websites that will specialize in your area of expertise. To do this just follow these instructions:

1 In the Google search box type article+keyword. So using our previous example we have typed "article+google book"

2 See if the sites you find will accept your article

The second option is the easiest way to distribute your articles, and that is to use article submission software. One submission service is available at www.articlesender.com

1 Navigate to www.articlesender.com

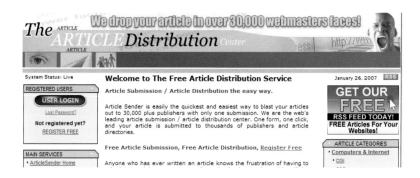

2 Click the link to Register Free

3 Fill out the Personal Information form and click Process Application

PERSONAL INFORMATION	
First Name:	
Last Name:	
Company Name:	
Street Address 1:	
Street Address 2:	
City:	
State:	
Zip Code:	
Country:	-- ▾
Phone Number:	
E-Mail Address:	

ARTICLE SENDER ACCOUNT INFORMATION	
Desired Username:	
Desired Password:	
Confirm Password:	

Process Application

Hot tip

Using article submission software will get your article distributed more easily and save you time.

4 You will now be able to submit your articles for free

Blogging

A blog is an online journal that people use like a diary to provide commentary or news on a particular subject. Blogs are becoming more and more common on the internet as they are a great way of keeping a record that everyone can access.

These can be very useful if you wish to keep people up to date as to what is going on in your business. You can even allow people to comment or add their own entries to your blog.

By having a current blog about your niche subject you can generate large amounts of related content over time. This of course Google loves as it feeds on good content.

If you would like to get a blog for your website you have two options:

- Use an external blog solution
- Install your own blog software

You can get an external blog that you can use via sites like www.blogger.com, which you set up like a web-based mail account.

Get your free blogger account

1 Sign in to your Google Account

2 Navigate to www.blogger.com

3 Click Create Your Blog Now

4 Your details will have been uploaded automatically. Create a display name and enter it in the box provided. Then click Continue

① Sign up for **Blogger**

Once you complete this process, you'll be able to log in to Blogger using your Google account email and password.

Email address	XXXXXXXXXXXXXXXXXXXXX	Use a different account
Your name	XXXXXXXXXXXXXXXXXXXXXXXXX	
Display name		The name used to sign your blog posts.
Acceptance of Terms	☐ I accept the Terms of Service	Indicate that you have read and understand Blogger's Terms of Service

CONTINUE

5 Enter a relevant name for your blog and the link name you wish to use. Then click Continue

② **Name** your blog

Blog title		Google Book	Enter a title for your blog.
Blog address (URL)		http://ineasystepsbook .blogspot.com Check Availability	You and others will use this to read and link to your blog.
Word Verification		mxVrt	Type the characters you see in the picture.
OR			
Advanced Setup		Want to host your blog somewhere else? Try Advanced Blog Setup. This will allow you to host your blog somewhere other than Blogspot.	

CONTINUE

6 Select the template you would like to use. Then click Continue

② Choose a **template**

CONTINUE

7 Click Start Posting to enter your blog

❗ Your **blog** has been created!

We have just created a blog for you. You can now add your posts to it, create your personal profile, or customise how your blog looks.

START POSTING

...cont'd

You can get some free blog software that you can install on your web server and set up so that you have total control over it, from www.wordpress.org

1 Navigate to www.wordpress.org

2 Select the Download link

3 Click Download .ZIP

4 Click Open to start downloading the software

10 Monitoring your results

It is essential to monitor your optimization results so that you know what is working and what needs more attention. This involves keeping your website up to date and current so that Google will crawl it more regularly.

Checking your web statistics

Every website should have its own site statistics package running as a standard feature.

This will feed back basic yet invaluable information about your website's performance and your visitors. This will help you to determine what is working and what you need to alter in order to increase your website's visitors. It will include such information as:

- Number of website visits

- Visit duration

- Countries your visitors are coming from

- When the search engines visit your website

- Most popular pages

- Entry pages

- Exit pages

- Time spent on pages

- What operating system your visitors are using

- What browser they are using

- What keywords your visitors used to find you

- What websites are sending visitors

- Links your website has gained and where they come from

- Any lost queries or problems with dead links

To access your website statistics you will need to find out the URL that you need to enter and any login procedure required to access it.

You should have received this information from your website host. If you had your website built for you by a company then you should contact them to get it.

Don't forget

Web statistics show a true picture of how effective your optimization has been.

...cont'd

Your statistics will look something like this:

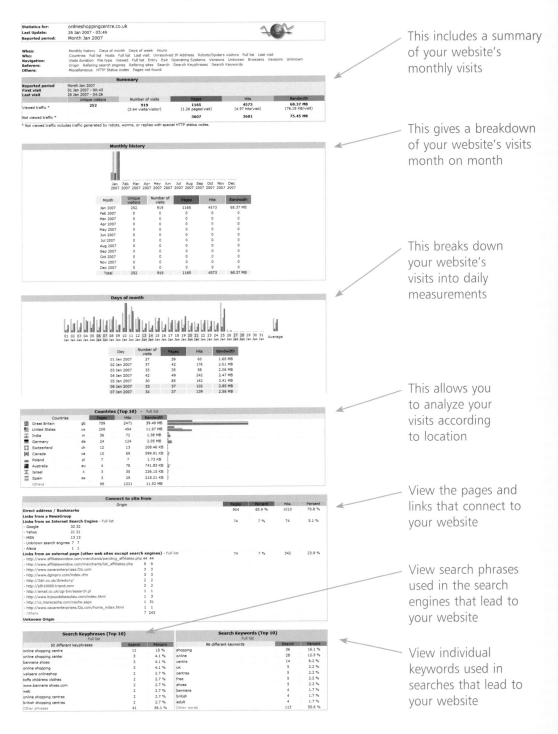

This includes a summary of your website's monthly visits

This gives a breakdown of your website's visits month on month

This breaks down your website's visits into daily measurements

This allows you to analyze your visits according to location

View the pages and links that connect to your website

View search phrases used in the search engines that lead to your website

View individual keywords used in searches that lead to your website

Using Google Analytics

Using your web statistics to tell you about your visitors is a good idea. Using Google Analytics to tell you everything you could possibly want to know about your visitors and website is a great idea.

Google Analytics can tell you nearly everything about your website. The main features we will use are the summary pages, and they are as follows:

- Executive overview
- Conversions summary
- Marketing summary
- Content summary
- Site overlay

Executive overview

- Site visits and page views
- New and returning visitors
- Geo Map overlay
- Visits by source

Hot tip

Use the Google Analytics goal tracking feature to monitor your conversions.

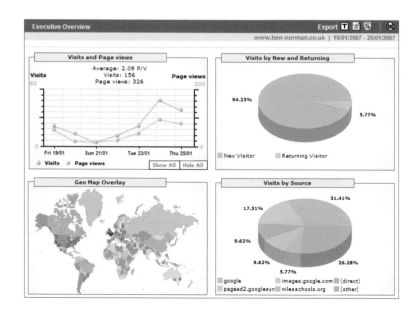

Conversion summary

- How many conversions you have had
- The ratio of conversions to visits

Conversion Summary			Export			
			www.ben-norman.co.uk	19/01/2007 - 25/01/2007		
Goal Conversion	Visits	%±	Conv. Rate %±			
1. Visits	156 ↑ 63%		100% — 0%			
2. G1: Newsletter Sign Up	0 — 0%		0% — 0%			
3. G2: Lead	2 ↑ 100%		1% ↑ 100%			

Help Information

Conversion Summary

Have my visits and conversion rates increased or decreased? This report shows whether the total number of visits, the number of conversions for each goal and the conversion rates for each goal have increased or decreased from a previous date range to the current date range. Define your starting (earliest) date range on the lower calendar, define your current or ending date range on the upper calendar.

- The first column (Visits) shows the total number of visits and the total number of conversions for each goal during the current date range (upper calendar). The green or red arrows and % numbers indicate the percentage increase or decrease in number of conversions respectively from the previous date range (lower calendar).
- The second column (Conv. Rate) shows the conversion rates for each goal for the current date range (upper calendar). The green or red arrows and % numbers indicate the percentage increase or decrease in the conversion rate from the earlier date range.

By monitoring the changes in conversion rates for your primary goals, you can monitor the overall effectiveness of website changes, marketing roll-outs and other events.

Conv. Rate is the number of goal conversions divided by visits.

Marketing summary top 5

- Referral sources
- Keywords
- Campaigns

Marketing Summary						Export		
					www.ben-norman.co.uk	19/01/2007 - 25/01/2007		
Top 5 Sources	Visits	%±	G1/Visit	%±	G2/Visit	%±		
1. google	49 ↑ 81%		0.00% — 0%		4.08% ↑ 100%			
2. images.google.com	27 ↑ 42%		0.00% — 0%		0.00% — 0%			
3. (direct)	15 ↑ 67%		0.00% — 0%		0.00% — 0%			
4. pagead2.googlesyndication.com	15 ↑ 100%		0.00% — 0%		0.00% — 0%			
5. nilesschools.org	9 ↑ 100%		0.00% — 0%		0.00% — 0%			
Top 5 Keywords	Visits	%±	G1/Visit	%±	G2/Visit	%±		
1. seo	5 ↓ -17%		0.00% — 0%		0.00% — 0%			
2. google consultant	5 — 0%		0.00% — 0%		0.00% — 0%			
3. website submission	3 ↑ 100%		0.00% — 0%		33.33% ↑ 100%			
4. submit website	3 ↑ 100%		0.00% — 0%		0.00% — 0%			
5. ben norman	2 ↓ -50%		0.00% — 0%		0.00% — 0%			
Top 5 Campaigns	Visits	%±	G1/Visit	%±	G2/Visit	%±		
1. (referral)	77 ↑ 54%		0.00% — 0%		0.00% — 0%			
2. (organic)	64 ↑ 73%		0.00% — 0%		3.13% ↑ 100%			
3. (direct)	15 ↑ 67%		0.00% — 0%		0.00% — 0%			

...cont'd

Content summary top 5

- Entrance pages

- Exit pages

- Content pages

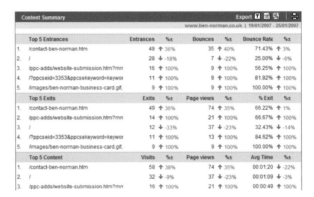

The site overlay

This will show you the most popular places within your website and will help you better understand the way your visitors are navigating through your website.

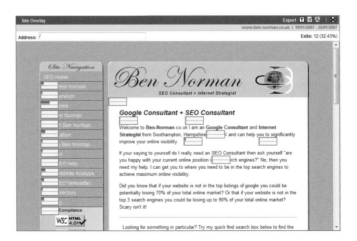

We have only covered the basic functions of Google Analytics here: there are many other features available.

Running ranking reports

Running ranking reports will feed back valuable information to you regarding where your website is currently ranked in Google's natural listings. Running a ranking report will also help you to identify the following information:

- The keywords for which you have successfully optimized your website

- The keywords for which you need to do more optimization work

- Which keywords are responsible for the traffic you are receiving

Run your ranking report

1. Open Web ceo and select Check Rankings

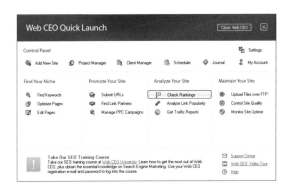

2. Select the website you require from the list provided or click New Site to add a new site

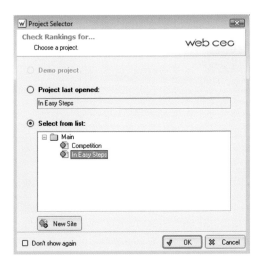

Don't forget

Run your reports regularly to monitor your search engine positions.

...cont'd

3 Click Configure and select the search engines for which you wish to check your ranking results

Use Web ceo to run your reports automatically at intervals that suit you.

Number your keywords to prioritize the order in which they are checked.

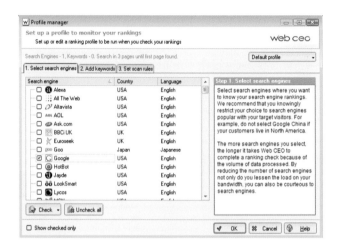

4 Select the "Add keywords" tab and then click the Add button. Click "Get keywords from site"

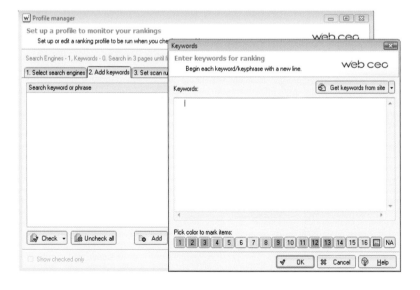

5 Check the box to enable Web ceo to crawl the top level of your website. This will automatically add in all of your used keywords for you. Then click OK

6 The keywords from your website will now be shown in the box. Double-check that these are correct and click OK

7 Now select the "Set scan rules" tab

Hot tip

Scan the top-level Meta data to ensure all of your keywords are included.

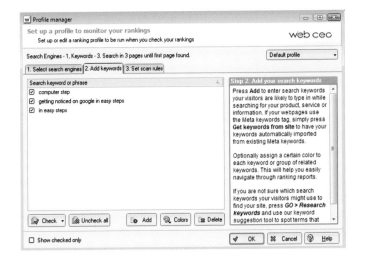

...cont'd

(8) Here you can define your scan rules if they are different from the default ones selected. Then click OK

Hot tip

Do not include sponsored results as you only want to view your natural results.

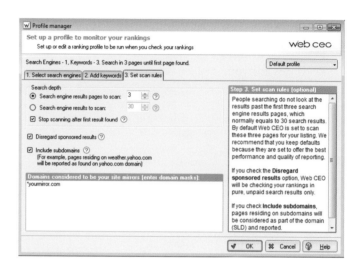

(9) Now select Start to begin the results process

Beware

Do not scan too many pages or it will take too long to run your report.

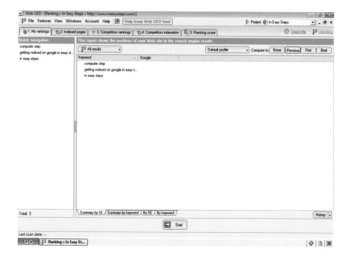

Web ceo will now go and query the requested search engines for your specific keyword phrases. It will provide information as to whether your website is ranked within those search engines and if so where.

Analyzing ranking reports

Once you have created your ranking report you need to analyze the data to see what the changes you have made have achieved.

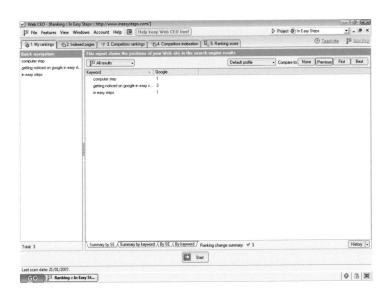

Don't forget

Positions will move around from time to time.

When you look at the report generated, you will be able to see and arrange your data in many different ways to enable you to get the most from it.

Your ranking report will tell you many things at a glance including:

- Pages added
- Pages removed
- Places gained
- Places dropped
- Ranked pages

This is done by selecting the relevant tabs at the bottom of the results window.

When you are analyzing your data you must always think about what you have done to your website so that you know to what changes to attribute your new results.

Don't forget

You may see different results in your ranking report to your browser if you are querying different data centers.

Site analysis

When your positions change for the worse it is a sign that your website is not staying current and is losing the relevance battle with Google.

To combat this and establish what needs to be done to regain your lost places, it is advisable to run regular analysis on your website's pages.

You should be running analysis on your page at least once per month but it is preferable to do this weekly.

Beware

Run regular analysis of your website to ensure you are keeping up to date with Google's algorithm.

132

Re-run your site analysis report

1 Open Web ceo and select Optimize Pages from the Find Your Niche category

2 Upload your website information by clicking Add website

3 Select the Optimization Advice and Analysis tab

4 Web ceo will have remembered the details of your last report so you simply need to click Start to produce your new report

Link analysis

As you have seen previously, links play an important part in the optimization process and you should pay close attention to how many links you have secured.

There are two ways in which to check this with ease:

Ask Google

Navigate to your home page and use the Google toolbar to tell you who points to your website:

Hot tip

You can also check your backward links from the Google toolbar.

1 Navigate to your website

2 Right-click on this page and select the Backward Links option from the Page Info category

3 Google will now display a list of your current inward links

In Easy Steps: Web Graphics in easy steps
About the author. Mary Lojkine has been writing about computers and technology for more than a decade. Her areas of expertise include the Internet, ...
www.ineasysteps.com/books/details/?1840782315 - 16k - Cached - Similar pages

In Easy Steps: Tell a friend
Tell a friend. Fill in this form and submit it to your friend. You can edit the message text if you wish. Your friend will then receive the information as ...
www.ineasysteps.com/site/tell/?1840782714 - 15k - Cached - Similar pages

4 You should now compare these with your previous list of inward links to see what links you have gained

...cont'd

Use Web ceo

This is particularly useful as it allows you to see why you are doing well with certain keywords.

1 Open Web ceo and click Analyze Link Popularity

Don't forget

You need to pay close attention not only to the number of links but to the anchor text used.

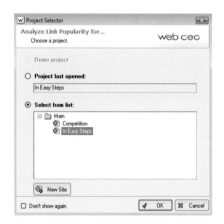

2 Select your site from the drop-down list and click OK

3 Click Configure and select the search engines you wish to query

4 Select the "Add pages" tab and select "Get URLs from site"

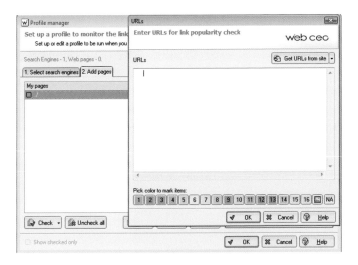

5 Select the depth of scan you want and click OK

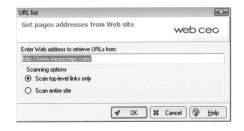

6 Click OK to accept the URLs found from your website

Hot tip

Using Web ceo will automate the process of tracking your links and also tell you your links for each page.

...cont'd

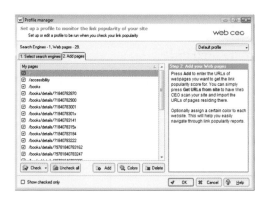

7 Click OK to confirm the uploaded links

Hot tip

If you notice a page has picked up a large number of links then use the Google toolbar to see who they are from.

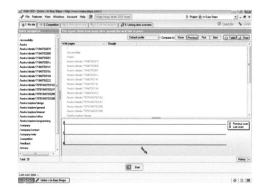

8 Click Start to run the report

9 Web ceo will now query the selected search engines and display its findings

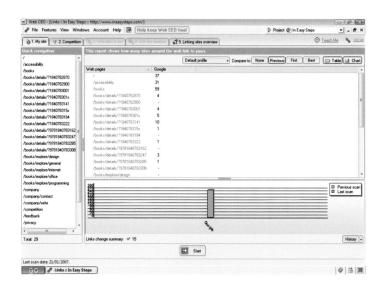

Competition analysis

In order to get to and remain at the top of the search results for your desired search terms, it is essential that you keep an eye on your competition.

Your top-ranked competition hold the key to achieving top results in Google and, as previously mentioned, to achieve the top position in Google you simply need to make your website more relevant in Google's eyes than theirs.

Monitoring your competition lets you know:

- What they are doing to their websites
- If their positions have changed
- What they are doing right
- What they are doing wrong

This will aid you to optimize your website further and keep one step ahead of your competition.

To analyze your competition we are going to analyze our webpage against theirs again to see what has changed.

To analyze and compare your website to your competitor's website follow the instructions starting on page 45.

Hot tip

Analyzing your competition will ensure that you always know what they are doing and how.

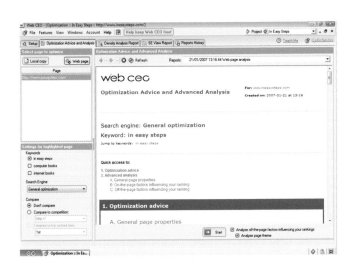

Keeping up to date

You will undoubtedly be making regular adjustments to your website and adding new content to keep it current.

It is very important therefore not to forget that you must keep everything else up to date. This will ensure that there are no loose ends and that everything is saying the same thing. This is crucial as you do not want your sitemap saying that old pages are there when you have removed them.

Potential problems

- Causing errors when your sitemap is crawled

- Giving Google incorrect information

- Creating inconsistencies in your website's structure

What to update

- Update the website sitemap

- Update the Google sitemap

- Update the website navigation

- Install the Google analytics code for the page

- Update your Google AdWords campaign (see page 142)

- Update keywords in the ranking checker tool

Google can tell how often your website is updated, and if it is updated often Google will most likely check it more often.

Google prefers websites that are updated regularly as the content they display is likely to be more up to date and relevant than content on websites that are updated less frequently.

This is a benefit for you as it means you will not have to wait as long to see the effects of your optimization efforts – meaning less waiting in between changes.

This will also help Google realize your relevance and begin to see your website as a reliable and up-to-date source of information on your niche subject.

Hot tip

If Google sees that your website is updated regularly it will begin to check it more regularly.

138

Adding new pages

If you are to have a successful and relevant website you will more than likely be adding new content regularly.

Adding content is great for your relevance as it gives Google more to assess and find relevance in.

When adding new content ensure

- You know what keywords you are targeting with it

- You add the new keywords to your ranking tool so that it will monitor their positions

- You put them in the appropriate place

- You have updated your sitemap and the Google sitemap

- You have used appropriate anchor text for the internal links to the page

The most important thing to do when adding new content is to make sure you know what keywords you are targeting with the new pages.

This will ensure that your content stays focused and includes your desired keywords. If your content does not include your keywords then it will not be very easy for Google to find its relevance.

When adding the new pages ensure

- Your keywords are used in the content

- You are also using semantically similar words

- You have related keywords in the internal links that point to the page

- Your keywords are in the Alt tags

- Your keywords are in the Meta and Title tags

By doing the above you will ensure that you have given Google the greatest help you can in assessing the relevance of your new web pages. This will not only help Google to assess what your pages are about, it will also ensure you will rank as highly as you possibly can with them.

Hot tip

Ensure your page name makes use of the main keywords for the page.

Beware

If you do not use your keywords in your new pages you will stand little chance of ranking well for them.

Don't forget

See chapter 6 for more information on adding new pages.

Removing content

At some point in time you will need to remove a page on your website.

This is an easy enough operation in itself but you must ensure that you update the site to reflect the fact that the page is no longer present.

If you fail to do so your visitors could end up just seeing this, and navigating away from your website:

What to do before removing content

- Remove all links to and references to the page

- Update your website's sitemap

- Update your Google sitemap

- Set up a 301 redirect to the new or most relevant page

What to check after you remove the page from your website

- Make sure your redirect is working by entering the URL for the old page and ensuring you are redirected to the new page

- If anyone was linking to the old page, contact them and ask them to update their link

When emailing people who had linked to the old page, ask them to amend the link to go to a new page on your website so as to ensure that the PageRank is passed on.

Beware

If you have dead links on your website it will affect your navigation and the quality of the visit for both Google and your human visitors.

11 Google AdWords

Google AdWords is your key to instant online visibility. You can pick specific keywords to target and have your website appearing for them in under an hour.

What is Google AdWords?

Google AdWords is a pay-per-click program run by Google.

What this means is that instead of earning positions as in the natural listings you can pay to be seen.

Google divides its search engine real estate into two parts:

- Natural listings
- Sponsored listings

Natural listings as you know cannot be bought, only earned through relevance, so good positions in them are only achievable through optimizing your website.

By using Google AdWords you will be appearing in the sponsored listings that are displayed alongside the natural listings by agreeing to pay if someone clicks on your ads.

At first this sounds very expensive but if managed correctly the costs involved are very reasonable considering the visibility and targeted traffic you will receive.

You will only have to pay a fee when you receive clicks on your advert. This means that you will only pay when Google sends someone to your website. The price of your clicks will vary depending on the industry you are in and the competition bidding on your specific keywords.

Don't forget

Google AdWords will only be cost-effective if set up and managed correctly.

Sponsored listings

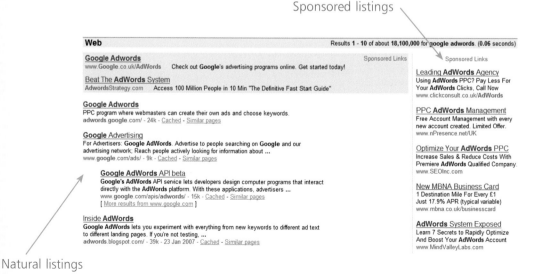

Natural listings

What are the benefits?

Google AdWords is a very important tool in your online marketing arsenal.

The reason this is such an important tool is that you can be on the first page of Google within just minutes of opening your AdWords account. Not only this, but you can actually choose the keywords for which you wish to appear when users search.

With AdWords you can create your advert and choose your keywords, save them and then be seen on Google within minutes. This is unlike optimizing your website, where you have to wait for the search engines to update and continually optimize for better results.

Google AdWords benefits

- Reach out to over 80% of internet users

- Target specific countries or areas

- Gain an instant Google position

- Choose your own keywords

- Create your own ad

- Split test ads to increase efficiency

- Decide which page to take the searchers to

- Track conversions

- Make instant changes to increase conversions

- Select a daily budget

The main benefit with using AdWords is that you can instantly appear under your desired keywords and have your website seen by people who are interested in what you are offering.

This makes the sales process easier as you do not have to convince people to buy what you are selling – they are already looking for it.

This ensures that your conversion rates will be higher than if you target people at random with other forms of advertising.

Beware

If your ads are not set up to be relevant, your campaign will not be financially efficient.

AdWords online coverage

The main reason to choose Google AdWords for your pay-per-click is the efficiency.

The second reason to choose Google AdWords is down to the online coverage that it has.

By placing your ad on Google AdWords and its partners you can potentially reach over 80% of the internet.

Where are Google ads displayed?

- Google
- AOL
- Netscape
- CompuServe
- Earth link
- ASK
- Shopping.com
- AT&T Worldnet
- What you need to know About
- Lycos
- Nytimes.com
- Infospace
- Reed Business
- Food network.com
- How stuff works
- Business.com
- HGTV

This offers you the great benefit of being able to get your website noticed by the people who are looking for it.

Don't forget

Google not only displays ads on Google – they appear on its partner sites too.

Setting up your account

To set up your Google AdWords account just follow the simple steps below:

1 Log in to your Google account and select Optimize Pages from the Find Your Niche category

My services - Edit

AdWords

Analytics

Local Business Center

Personalized Homepage - Add content

2 Select the AdWords link

Don't forget

You can also log in from the Google AdWords page.

3 Now click "Start now"

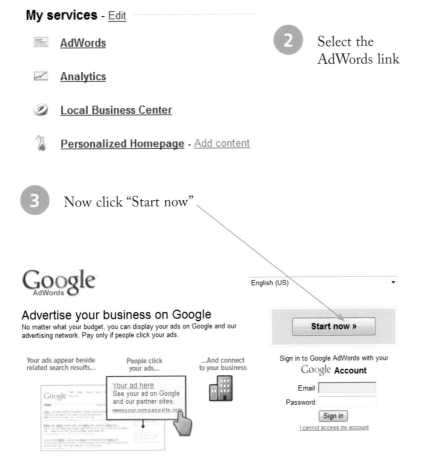

...cont'd

4 Select the Standard Edition option and click Continue

5 Select your preferred language and how you wish to target your customers (we will be targeting by country)

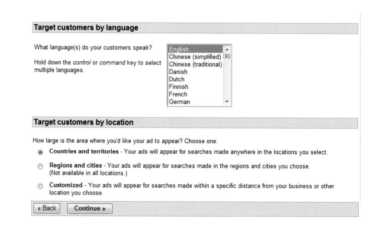

6 Select the countries where you wish to have your ads shown

Target customers by country or territory

Highlight the countries or territories on the left where you'd like your ad to appear, then click 'Add.' Select as many as you like. Your ads will appear to users anywhere in each location you select.

Available Countries and Territories

Turkmenistan
Turks and Caicos Islands
Tuvalu
Uganda
Ukraine
United Arab Emirates
United Kingdom
United States
United States Minor Outlying Islands
Uruguay

Add »
« Remove

Selected Countries and/or Territories

United States

« Back   Continue »

Writing the perfect ad

The secret of a great-performing AdWords campaign lies not only in the selection of the keywords but also in the creation of an effective advert.

When people select an advert to click on they are weighing up many different factors before they click on it. The main thing they are looking for is relevance and this is something that you need to ensure that they can see.

Bad Ad

<u>in easy steps</u>
**book about google search engine
and how to get high in it**
www.ineasysteps.com/books

Good Ad

<u>Google Book</u>
Increase your Positions on Google
Instantly Download your copy Now
www.ineasysteps.com/GoogleBook

Remember you need to create individual ad groups for each of your products or services. This will enable you to target each area specifically, which will increase the relevance of each of your ads.

This in turn will increase your conversion rates and the efficiency of your campaign. Do not be tempted to create just one ad for all of your keywords as it will not be as efficient or cost-effective.

Ensure your ad:

- Does not use your company name in the title
- Includes your keywords
- Mentions a benefit
- Capitalizes on important words

Beware

Do not include things like telephone numbers in your ad as its only job is to encourage people to click on it.

Dynamic titles

The first and most important part of your ad is the title.

Your ad's title is used to grab the attention of the searcher and it needs to do this by being as relevant as possible.

Dynamic titles do just that: they are dynamic and will adjust to mimic the searcher's phrase as long as it is present among your keywords. This means that when a searcher looks for one of your keywords, not only will the ad show but the title will be shouting relevance at them.

Google helps with this as it will highlight the keywords in your ad as well, all of which will further help your ad to stand out.

To implement a dynamic title you simply need to add the following code to your AdWords title, using your own keyword:

```
{KeyWord:insert keywords}
```

Now that you have added this to your title, the ad will display the searcher's exact search phrase as your title if you have it among your keywords. (These are your keywords for your AdWords advert, not your website.)

Now that your ad has a dynamic title your ads will start to mimic the keywords searched for, as shown below:

Hot tip

Dynamic titles will ensure your ad is always as relevant as it can be.

Dynamic title

<u>Google Books</u>
Increase your Positions on Google
Instantly Download your copy Now

This would be your ad when users search for Google Books.

If the searcher looks for a keyword that matches one of yours broadly but not exactly, your ad will still show but it will display as shown below using your generic title text, which in this example is "Google Book".

Normal title

<u>Google Book</u>
Increase your Positions on Google
Instantly Download your copy Now

Body with action

The body of your Google AdWords ad should always do two things.

The first is to show relevance to the searcher. The second is to tell the searcher what to do next. These two things are imperative for a well-performing ad. This is the main reason for writing new ads for each of your products or services.

The first line of your ad should be used to capture the interest of searchers and show them the benefits of what you are offering.

Examples of a good capture line would be:

- Increase your profits

- Lower your recruitment costs

- Stop cats coming into your garden

The second line of your ad should be used to tell the person reading what they should do.

Examples of some good "call to action" lines would be:

- Get your free report now

- Instant download available

- See how online now

You can also add certain words that will make your ad more appealing such as:

- Free

- Secret

- Instant download

- Cheapest available

Beware

Do not use capitalization excessively or Google will reject your ads. Only capitalize important words.

Body created properly

Google Book
Increase your Positions on Google
Instantly Download your copy Now

URLs

Your URL is also an important part of your ad and can be used to add relevance.

With the URL part of your ad you can select both the URL text that is seen and the page the searcher is taken to on selecting your ad.

Your destination URL and the display URL do not and should not be the same.

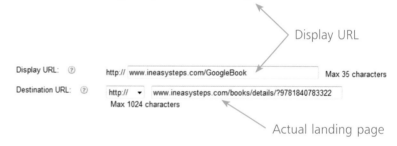

Display URL

Actual landing page

The display URL is not the URL of the page that the searcher will be taken to but it will help to build in some more relevance and so will help us.

It is also important to note that you should not always take the searcher to your home page. In fact the home page is usually a page you would not want to take a searcher to.

You should try and take the searcher to the most relevant page on your website to further increase the relevance for them of clicking on your ad.

If the ad is for a "Google book" and you have a bookshop full of books you would want to send that searcher directly to the page on your website that describes the "Google book".

This helps to confirm to the searcher that they have made the right decision and will help them to find what they were looking for more quickly, without having to search for it.

Keyword features

Google AdWords not only allows you to choose the keywords for which you wish to appear, but also gives you tools to help you control how broad or concise you need them to be.

These tools are called keyword matching options. There are four different types of keyword matching options. They will allow you to focus your keywords better.

▼ Advanced option: match types
Use these formats to make your keywords more precise [?]

```
keyword   = broad match
[keyword] = exact match
"keyword" = phrase match
-keyword  = negative match
```

Broad match

This is the default option when you implement your keywords. The broad match option means that whenever a search is made that contains all of your specific keywords, your ad will be shown.

"Phrase match"

This option means that your ad will only be shown if your keywords are searched for in the order you have written them. Your ad will still appear if other keywords are present in the query but only if yours are in order and together.

[Exact match]

This option means that your ad will only be shown when your exact search phrase is searched for.

-Negative match

This option is used when there are specific keywords for which you do not want your ad to appear. Most businesses would use −free as a negative keyword as people searching for a free version of what they are selling would not be useful visitors.

The use of these keyword matching options can help you reduce your unwanted and unprofitable clicks, which will help to increase your return on investment (ROI).

Choosing your keywords

Your keywords are the words for which you wish to have this particular ad shown.

It is important to remember that you will need to create separate ads for each service or product so you should only enter keywords that are specific to this ad.

When selecting keywords remember to make use of the keywords you have previously identified from your keyword research and analysis.

To choose your keywords you have several options:

- Enter specific phrases

- Find related keywords by using the search facility

- Scan Google's suggested categories based on a scan of your website

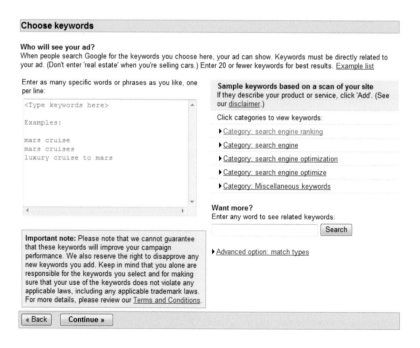

Once you have decided on your keywords, select Continue to move to the next step.

Selecting your budget

1 You now need to set up your daily budget and your maximum cost per click

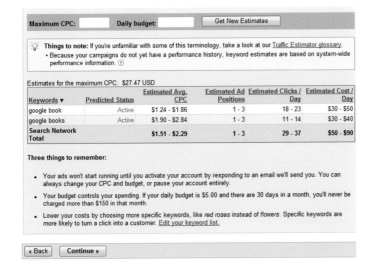

2 Now enter your desired amount and see how many clicks Google thinks it can deliver you per day

Maximum CPC:		Daily budget:		Get New Estimates

Things to note: If you're unfamiliar with some of this terminology, take a look at our Traffic Estimator glossary.
• Because your campaigns do not yet have a performance history, keyword estimates are based on system-wide performance information.

Estimates for the maximum CPC: $27.47 USD

Keywords ▼	Predicted Status	Estimated Avg. CPC	Estimated Ad Positions	Estimated Clicks / Day	Estimated Cost / Day
google book	Active	$1.24 - $1.86	1 - 3	18 - 23	$30 - $50
google books	Active	$1.90 - $2.84	1 - 3	11 - 14	$30 - $40
Search Network Total		$1.51 - $2.29	1 - 3	29 - 37	$50 - $90

Three things to remember:

• Your ads won't start running until you activate your account by responding to an email we'll send you. You can always change your CPC and budget, or pause your account entirely.

• Your budget controls your spending. If your daily budget is $5.00 and there are 30 days in a month, you'll never be charged more than $150 in that month.

• Lower your costs by choosing more specific keywords, like *red roses* instead of *flowers*. Specific keywords are more likely to turn a click into a customer. Edit your keyword list.

[« Back] [Continue »]

153

Reviewing your account

1 You now need to go through, review and accept your account

2 Select your preferred option and click Continue

3 Select the radio button that says you already have an account you wish to use, to link your AdWords account to your Google account. You will then see the Google account login box where you will need to enter your account details and click Continue

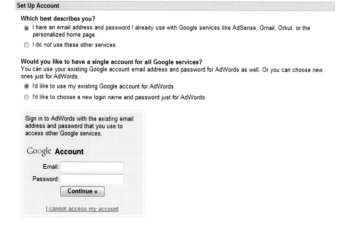

4 Your AdWords account will now have been created and you need to log in to activate it

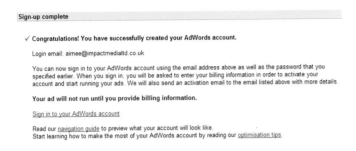

Hot tip

By using your Google account details you will save time and be able to keep all your accounts together.

5 To activate your new account you must enter your payment information by clicking Billing Preferences

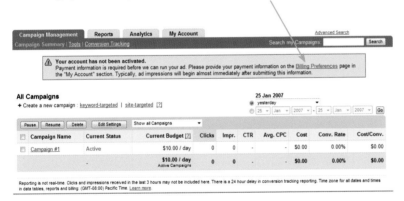

6 Enter your location details, your specific time zone and give a promotional code if you have one

Beware

Ensure you select the right location-specific details as failure to do so may result in your account not activating.

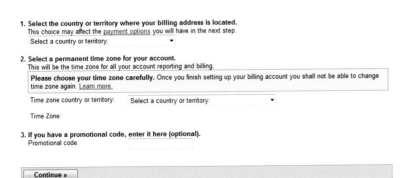

...cont'd

7 Select your preferred payment method and click Continue

Account Setup

Select location > **Choose form of payment** > Agree to terms > Provide billing details

Tell us how you would like to pay for your ads.
Given your currency and billing address location, only one form of payment is available at this time. If your billing country or territory is flexible, additional forms of payment may be available to you. To change your options, go back and select another country or territory.

Post-pay Billing - After you receive clicks, we automatically charge your card or account.
○ Credit Card	American Express, MasterCard, JCB, Visa, and debit cards with a MasterCard or Visa logo

Note: You will pay Google AdWords for the ads that you run. For details, read 'Understanding AdWords'.

[« Back] [Continue »]

8 Read through Google's terms and conditions and click Yes if you agree, and then Continue

Google Ireland Limited Programme Service Agreement (the "Service Agreement")

This Agreement (as defined below) is entered into by you, being either an advertising third party or an Advertiser and being either: (i) the party which accepts this Agreement online and is listed on the account you create; or (ii) being the entity identified as the "Bill To" on the Front Page (if any) of this Agreement which signs this Agreement (**"Customer"** / **"You"**) and Google Ireland Limited (registered number: 368047) with its registered office located at 1st and 2nd Floor, Gordon House, Barrow Street, Dublin 4, Ireland (**"Google"**).

1. Definitions
"Acceptance Date" means either: (i) the date on which Customer accepts this Agreement online; or (ii) the acceptance date listed on the signatory page (if any) of this Agreement;
"Advertiser" means the entity whose ads (whether created by itself or by a third party on its behalf) are made available by Google in accordance with this Agreement, which entity may be more particularly detailed on the Front Page (if any) of this Agreement;
"AdWords Progamme" means Google's online auction based advertising programme;
"Agreement" means these advertising terms and conditions (including the Front Page and the signatory page if any), the FAQs and the Editorial Guidelines;
"Creatives" means all ad content (including without limitation any URLs, all contact information and/or other data in the ad) which are subject to the Editorial Guidelines;
"Editorial Guidelines" means the Programme's (i) text ad editorial guidelines located at: https://adwords.google.co.uk/select/guidelines.html; (ii) image ad editorial guidelines located at https://adwords.google.co.uk/select/imageguidelines.html; and (iii) such other editorial guidelines relating to different types of ads located at such URL(s) as made available to You from time to time;
"End Date" means the date (if any) on which the parties agree this Agreement will terminate and all types of ads will cease to be

○ Yes, I agree to the above terms and conditions.

Please read about how credit card payment works.
• Your ads will start running on Google right away. When your advertising charges reach a preset amount, your credit card is automatically charged. You will not be notified, so be sure to check back on the 'Billing Summary' page for charges.
• To keep your ads running, be sure your card information is up-to-date on the 'Billing Preferences' page.
• You can change your credit card at any time.

Enter your credit card information.
Type of card: select card type ▾

Provide your billing address.
Contact name:
Company name:
Address line 1:
Address line 2:
City:
County:
Postcode:
Country/Territory: United States   Not your billing country or territory?
                                        You must select another form of payment
Telephone number:
Fax number:

9 Input your details. Your account will then be activated and your ad will go live

Select your primary business type. Please choose one, either from the first box or the second
Business to Business (B2B)   Business to Consumer (B2C)
------ select a B2B type ------ ▾ - or - ------ select a B2C type ------ ▾

Your account will be charged a USD $5.00 activation fee upon continuing.
[« Back] [Save and Activate]

12 Test and Measure

Running regular reports will ensure your AdWords account is staying efficient.

Landing pages

Landing pages can be very useful in conjunction with Google AdWords.

With AdWords you can select the page you want the ad to point to, so you are not at Google's mercy as with the natural listings. To make the most of this you can create pages that are tailored to the searcher's specific query.

Effective landing pages

- Be relevant to the searcher's query

- Restrict navigation

- Speak to searchers, not at them

- Mention benefits

- Tell them what to do next

- Lead to purchase or enquiry

When you have created your new landing page you should use the Google ad split testing feature to test it and see whether it is more effective. This way you can modify the landing page again and again to make it more and more effective.

Landing page aims

- Get their contact details via a form

- Get them to make a purchase

If you can get searchers to do this you can measure your results and track them within AdWords. This will help you to work out how cost-effective your campaign is.

You really need to use your landing page to get the desired action, which will be different depending on what you are doing.

If you are selling products then you will be utilizing the landing page to make visitors purchase the item. If you are selling services then you will want to get their contact details because with these you will be able to contact the lead and start the sales process.

Do not make the mistake of always trying to go for a sale.

Conversion tracking

Conversion tracking is essential to be able to see how truly cost-effective your Google AdWords campaign is.

Only when you know this can you really start seeing what's what when it comes to your account. Conversion tracking will even tell you exactly how much each conversion is costing you so that you can work out your overheads.

Hot tip

Conversion tracking is a must for a financially efficient account as without it you have no idea what is resulting in leads or sales.

1 Log in to your Google account

2 Select AdWords from the services menu

3 Now select the Conversion Tracking link

4 Click Start Tracking Conversions

Beware

Your conversion tracking will not work if you do not implement the code correctly.

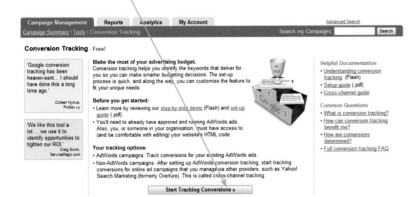

...cont'd

5 Now choose your conversion type. If you were selling a product or item then here you would normally select Purchase/Sale

Don't forget

You need to use the code relevant to the conversion type you have selected.

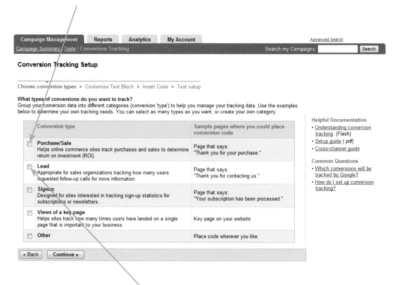

If you were selling a service then you would choose Lead. (Using our example of a Google book we will select Purchase/Sale.) Then click Continue

6 Here you can customize the text and color format, and a preview will be shown at the bottom of the page. Then click Continue

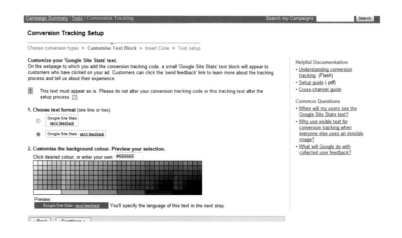

7 Enter your conversion language and security details. Now copy the code provided and paste it into your relevant conversion webpage(s)

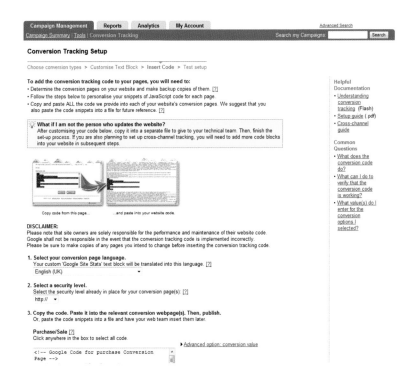

Hot tip

This enables you to see how efficient your campaign really is.

Beware

Ensure you get the right security details or the code will not work.

161

8 Your conversion tracking has now been set up. You can view this by navigating to your AdWords ad, or wait for a customer to complete a conversion

Don't forget

This will have added two new columns to your report allowing you to see how much your conversions are really costing you.

Split testing

Split testing ads is an important part of increasing your conversions and lowering your cost per conversion.

Google allows you to set up your ad group with multiple ads so you can play them off against each other to see which one gives you the best results.

This is a continual process and you should always be playing ads off against each other.

The way to do this is to create two ads that are slightly different. Google will then serve both ads and feed back the results of both, which will enable you to tell which one is performing the best.

You can use the new ads to split test:

- New destination URLs

- New ads

When you have decided which is the worse performing ad you need to assess why and then change it to try and make it more effective than the best performing ad. This is something that you will need to work on and it is a great way to ensure that your ads are always getting you the best response.

To start split testing your ads follow the steps below:

1 Navigate to the Campaign Management page and select the ad that you wish to split test

Click the campaign you want to split test from this list

2 Select the ad group you want to split test from your selected campaign

3 Select which type of ad you would like to create in order to split test them

4 You now have the option of changing the title and description or the destination URL. This decision depends on what you would like to split test: the implementation of new descriptions in your ad or the landing page to which your customers are directed

Hot tip

Ensure that you have conversion tracking set up to ensure that you are getting all of your data fed back.

Monitoring your results

Regular reports will help you to ensure that your figures are going in the right direction.

Google will allow you to create fully customized reports that will help you track things down to the minutest detail. Google will allow you to save the results and will allow you to run the reports automatically. You can also set up the reports to have Google email them to you when they are generated.

A very good report to generate is a daily account report, as seen below:

Hot tip

Regular reporting will help you maximize the efficiency of your account.

1 Navigate to the Campaign Management page and select the Reports tab

2 Select Create a Report Now

3 Select which type of report you would like to run (in this case we will select Account Performance)

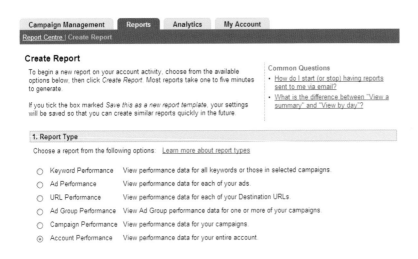

Beware

If you do not run regular reports you will be wasting money.

4 Now select the time and date settings for your report from the drop-down lists provided. This report is very useful as it allows you to view daily information about your ad's performance for the time that it has been live

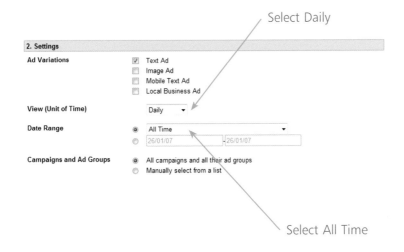

Select Daily

Select All Time

5 From the Advanced Settings category you need to select the Conversions, Conversion Rate and Cost/Conversion

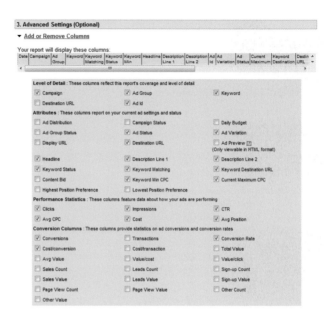

6 Select a name for your report and decide whether you want regular email reports sent

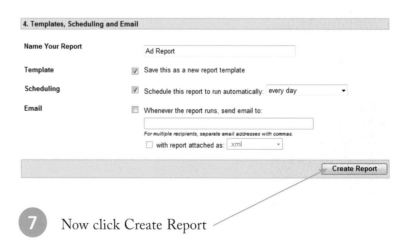

7 Now click Create Report

13 Froogle

Froogle is Google's product

search engine.

What is Froogle?

Froogle is a shopping search engine from Google that people can use to search specifically for products.

Froogle shows photographs of products related to the search query. Users can also restrict and modify their searches by:

● Price

● Type of goods

● Retailer

If you have got something to sell then Froogle may be for you. You can upload products and have them found on Froogle.

Froogle works in the same way Google does in that relevance achieves the highest positions.

The only difference with Froogle is that it is only interested in listing products.

Listing your products on Froogle will give you many benefits including:

● More coverage

● Extra chances to sell

● A product-only portal to advertise on

If you are selling products then you really need to have them listed on Froogle. This way you can be found in either Google or Froogle.

Add individual products

If you would like to add your individual product to Froogle follow the steps below:

 Navigate to the Froogle home page and select the Information for Sellers link

Web   Images   Video   News   Maps   **more »**

[Search Froogle]   Advanced Froogle Search
Preferences
Froogle Help

froo·gle (fru'gal) *n.* **Smart shopping through Google.**

A few of the items recently found with Froogle:

kiehl's	bumper sticker	lift chair	scissors	inflatable kayak
ski boots	cheese grater	gyroscope	club chair	patio heaters
samurai sword	miter saw	beard trimmer	robomower	dustbuster
sapphire pendant	paella pan	sea salt	fragrance	mini digital camera
food dehydrator	gps watch	softball bat	boonie hat	school supplies

Google Home - Information for Sellers - Froogle Tour - About Google

Hot tip

If you only have one or two products, this is how to add them.

169

 Select what you would like to sell from the drop-down menu

Google Sell with Google

Got something to sell? We can help make it happen – for free. Here's how.

1. **Post your items on Google Base so they'll be found on Google.**

   It costs nothing to reach shoppers by submitting your items to Google Base so they'll be found on Google (you'll be asked to create a Google account if you don't already have one). You can link directly from our search results to your website, and if you don't have one, we'll host your offers for free.

   From Google Base you can also create AdWords ads to advertise each of your offers.

   Get started and post your items now

   [Choose what you want to sell ▾]

   [Post one at a time] or [Bulk upload]

2. **Process online sales using Google Checkout.**

   Use Checkout to charge your customers' credit cards, process their orders and receive payment in your bank account.

   Google Checkout is even better for your bottom line if you use AdWords. For every $1 you spend as an AdWords advertiser, you can process $10 in transactions for free through Google Checkout. For example: if you spent $1,000 on AdWords last month, this month you can process $10,000 in sales for free.

   More on integrating Google Checkout with my existing site »
   More on using Google Checkout if I don't have my own site »

3 Select your item type from the drop-down menu. If it is not available then create your own

Hot tip

If your item type is not there create a new keyword-specific one.

4 For this example, we will select Products from the drop-down menu

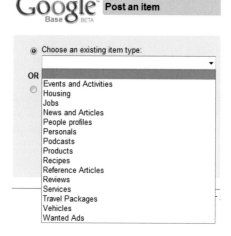

5 You can also upload multiple items with a bulk upload file. This will be explained in the next section

6 Fill in your product details and description, adding any additional points

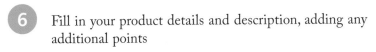

Title

Google Book

Details

Price: $ 20 per item
Number-unit

Price type: Fixed price
Text

Quantity: 1
Number

Product Type: Book   ▼ remove this
Text   e.g. "Jewelry"

Condition: New   ▼ remove this
Text   e.g. "New"

Brand: In Easy Steps   ▼ remove this
Text

Author: Ben Norman   ▼ remove this
Text

Include additional details for your item
(Click a field name to include it with your item.)

Apparel Type
Color
Model number
Size
UPC
Weight

Create your own...

Hot tip

Use additional details to add relevance when possible.

Description

⊖ Link | **B** *I* | ≡ T₂ | ≣ ≣ ≣ | *F* Font ▼ | ⫟T Size ▼ | Headings ▼   Edit HTML

Essential reading for anyone looking to successfully market their website on the search engine Google.

Getting noticed on Google in easy steps will carefully walk you through the processes of marketing a website to Google in easy-to-follow steps. Regardless of your level of skill you will be able to make positive changes to your website, enabling it to enter and climb the rankings of Google. This is essential information for all website owners as first page listings in Google are highly sought after. They are responsible for generating huge quantities of targeted traffic and revenue. This book contains specific information on how to identify the keywords being searched for, and how to identify niche markets with little or no competition. It then goes on to show how to implement the keywords in your website, making it highly relevant. There is also extensive information on improving existing Google positions and keeping ahead of your competition. Overall this book shows website owners how to successfully market their websites to Google, the world's most popular search engine.

7 If you wish to add a picture of your product then you can do this through one of the following options

Hot tip

When describing your product include your keywords to ensure it gets found for them.

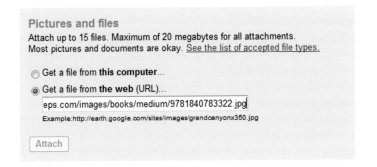

Pictures and files
Attach up to 15 files. Maximum of 20 megabytes for all attachments.
Most pictures and documents are okay. See the list of accepted file types.

○ Get a file from **this computer**...
◉ Get a file from **the web** (URL)...

eps.com/images/books/medium/9781840783322.jpg

Example:http://earth.google.com/sites/images/grandcanyonx350.jpg

[Attach]

...cont'd

8 Enter your contact details

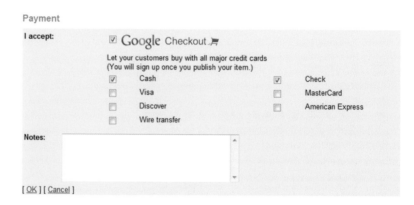

Contact

This will be published on the Internet.

Name: Ben Norman

Phone: 0845 3751756

[OK] [Cancel]

9 Enter your payment details and any additional notes

Don't forget

Your contact details will be shown on the internet.

Payment

I accept:

☑ **Google** Checkout

Let your customers buy with all major credit cards
(You will sign up once you publish your item.)

☑	Cash	☑	Check
☐	Visa	☐	MasterCard
☐	Discover	☐	American Express
☐	Wire transfer		

Notes:

[OK] [Cancel]

10 Enter your location and delivery details, adding any specific information if required

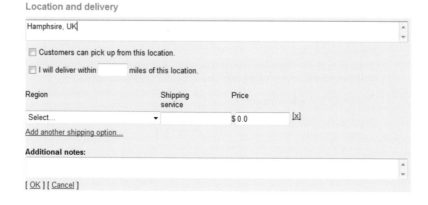

Location and delivery

Hamphsire, UK

☐ Customers can pick up from this location.

☐ I will deliver within ___ miles of this location.

Region	Shipping service	Price	
Select... ▼		$ 0.0	[x]

Add another shipping option...

Additional notes:

[OK] [Cancel]

11 If you wish to create a specific AdWords ad you can do so here

AdWords Ad

☑ Run this ad?

Your ad will appear on Google.com search results when someone searches for a related term. If you do not already have a
Google AdWords account, you will have to provide your billing information and agree to the AdWords Terms and Conditions.
Review our editorial guidelines.

Write your ad:

Google Book	25 characters max
Increase Your Positions on Google	35 characters max
Instantly Download Your Copy NOW	35 characters max

base.google.com

What is your maximum cost per click for this ad?
You only pay for an ad when a searcher clicks on it. You choose the maximum amount that you're willing to pay. The higher you
bid, the more likely your ad will appear next to search results for relevant queries.
How do I choose a max CPC?

I will pay at most $ 0.30   every time someone clicks on my ad.

Note: you will be able to set a maximum daily budget when you create your ads campaign.

[OK] [Cancel]

Hot tip

Create your ad in AdWords as you will be able to select the specific keywords you want.

If you decide to create and activate your AdWords ad at the same time as you add your product to Froogle, Google will show your ad for terms it believes to be relevant.

You can create an ad from your AdWords account in the same way but you will be able to select the keywords for which you wish it to appear.

 12 Preview your ad before making it live

Beware

Always preview your ad to ensure it is OK before publishing it.

See what your ad will look like before you go any further

Select this option to save your changes and list your product on Froogle

Preview	Save draft	Publish	Cancel

Save a copy of your ad for later

Select Cancel to return to the Froogle homepage without saving your ad

173

...cont'd

 If you are now happy with your ad, select Publish. If you would like to re-edit it, select Edit.

Google Book

Details

Price:	$ 20.00 per item
Quantity:	1
Product Type:	Book
Condition:	New
Brand:	In Easy Steps
Author:	Ben Norman

Description

Essential reading for anyone looking to successfully market their website on the search engine Google.

Getting noticed on Google in easy steps will carefully walk you through the processes of marketing a website to Google in easy-to-follow steps. Regardless of your level of skill you will be able to make positive changes to your website, enabling it to enter and climb the rankings of Google. This is essential information for all website owners as first page listings in Google are highly sought after. They are responsible for generating huge quantities of targeted traffic and revenue. This book contains specific information on how to identify the keywords being searched for, and how to identify niche markets with little or no competition. It then goes on to show how to implement the keywords in your website, making it highly relevant. There is also extensive information on improving existing Google positions and keeping ahead of your competition. Overall this book shows website owners how to successfully market their websites to Google, the world's most popular search engine.

Contact

Name:	Ben Norman
Phone:	0845 3751756

Payment

I accept:	Google Checkout, Cash, Check

This item will expire in 30 days.

Pictures

9781840783322.jpg - Download (6.64KB)

Location and delivery

Hampshire, UK

©2007 Google - Map data ©2007 TeleAtlas - Terms of Use
View Larger Map

Will ship to United Kingdom for $ 5.00

Hot tip

Always use a picture to ensure your ad is as visually appealing as possible.

You have now successfully submitted your product to Google's product search engine, Froogle.

If you wish to add further products you should follow the same process again, customizing it for the new products.

However, if you have many items and you have some technical knowledge it may be easier to use the bulk upload feature instead.

Add multiple products

If you have multiple products that you would like to upload at the same time you can do this via the bulk upload function available on Froogle.

You will need to have some basic technical knowledge to use this function as it involves the use of either:

● Tab-delimited spreadsheets

● XML

You can also purchase software that will give you a user-friendly interface to help you upload products to Froogle. Whether to do this is personal choice and would depend on:

● How many products you have to upload

● How much you would use the software

● Whether you could use the more technical methods

① Select Products from the drop-down list and then select "Bulk upload"

Google **Sell with Google**

Got something to sell? We can help make it happen – for free. Here's how.

① **Post your items on Google Base so they'll be found on Google.**
It costs nothing to reach shoppers by submitting your items to Google Base so they'll be found on Google (you'll be asked to create a Google account if you don't already have one). You can link directly from our search results to your website, and if you don't have one, we'll host your offers for free.

From Google Base you can also create AdWords ads to advertise each of your offers.

Get started and post your items now

Choose what you want to sell ▾

[Post one at a time] or [Bulk upload]

② **Process online sales using Google Checkout.**
Use Checkout to charge your customers' credit cards, process their orders and receive payment in your bank account.

Google Checkout is even better for your bottom line if you use AdWords. For every $1 you spend as an AdWords advertiser, you can process $10 in transactions for free through Google Checkout. For example: if you spent $1,000 on AdWords last month, this month you can process $10,000 in sales for free.

More on integrating Google Checkout with my existing site »
More on using Google Checkout if I don't have my own site »

...cont'd

 Select Products from the item type menu

Bulk upload files are classified according to what sort of information they contain, or *item type*. Each item type is associated with its own set of standard attributes, which define the characteristics of your items.

Select an item type below for sample bulk upload files and a list of appropriate attributes, which you will use to create your bulk upload.

Popular Item Types

Most information in Google Base falls into one of the following item types:

Events and activities Events and activities to attend	**Recipes** Instructions for creating culinary dishes
Housing Individual properties for sale or rent	**Reviews** Evaluations of products and media
Jobs Individual employment opportunities	**Services** Available services
Personals People seeking people	**Travel packages** Trips and accommodations offered
Products	**Vehicles**

Hot tip

Use the file template to make your life easier and save time.

 Create your file from one of the sample files and then select the "register your bulk upload" link

Creating your bulk upload

We accept bulk uploads in five formats, including tab-delimited and four XML formats: RSS 2.0, RSS 1.0, Atom 1.0, and Atom 0.3. If you're uncertain about which format you should use, please see our bulk upload format page.

We've provided sample files to illustrate how your bulk upload file should be formatted. You can download a sample in any of these formats, and use it as a template for your own bulk upload file. For tab-delimited, the sample is available as both a text file (.txt) and a Microsoft Excel spreadsheet (.xls).

Tab-delimited	RSS 1.0	RSS 2.0	Atom 0.3	Atom 1.0
Sample (.txt) Sample (.xls)	Sample	Sample	Sample	Sample

Whichever format you choose, you'll need to provide information about your products in the form of attributes. Organizing your content into attributes will enable people to search for it on Google Base. We've listed the required attributes below.

Once you've created a file with the set of attributes which best describe your products, you can register your bulk upload.

You now will have two ways to upload your file:

- Upload it via Google Base
- Upload it via FTP

Note that if your file is over 20 MB you will have to upload it via the FTP method. The file upload may take several minutes and you will be notified when it has been successful.

14 Extra help

Hiring a specialist

Sometimes you will want to hire a specialist to ensure that your site is working to the best of its ability.

Reasons to hire a specialist

- You need extra help because your industry is very competitive

- You do not have time

- It would work out more expensive for you to do it yourself

The last option is the most common reason and yet the most often overlooked. There is a misconception that if you do things yourself it will work out cheaper.

This is not always the case as you need to assess how much your time is worth. You must then look at how long it will take you to optimize your website and work out whether you would earn more money doing other work in that amount of time.

It can sometimes be financially beneficial for you to earn more money in the same time doing what you do and pay a specialist to take care of the optimization of your website.

It is important therefore that you hire the correct person for the job. By the correct person we mean someone who knows what they are doing and who will only use ethical means.

Before you hire anyone to work on the optimization of your website make sure that they can give you the correct answers to the following questions:

- Do you only perform ethical optimization?

- Can I see some examples of your work?

- What places have you achieved for your clients?

- Do you optimize for keywords that bring real traffic?

- Will I get a report to explain what has been done?

- Will I need a monthly package to maintain my results?

- Will I be able to contact you when and as I need to?

- Do you have a client I could contact as a reference?

Don't forget

Specialists will be busy and you may have to wait a month or so for them to start work on your website.

178

As in any industry there are some unscrupulous companies and so-called specialists who will try to con you with different tricks such as:

Top ten listings but no traffic

This is a common trick used and one that is normally not noticed until it is too late. Site owners get so fixated with top ten listings that they can neglect to check whether people actually search for the keywords.

To combat this ask the specialist whether you will receive a report outlining the keywords to be used and the expected monthly searches.

Hiding text on the page

Sometimes companies will hide text on your page to try and increase the relevance of the page. This does not work as Google can tell if the color of the text is the same as the background. If Google detects this you will be penalized and possibly removed from the search listings.

To ensure this has not happened to you, navigate to your page and choose Select All from the Edit menu on your browser.

Optimizing their own website with your money

Creating new and optimized sites is a tactic used to increase the dependency of your website. This is achieved by increasing the PageRank of the new website and linking into your website from it. This in itself is OK but you must check that you own the website that they are working on. If you don't, you will be paying the company to optimize a site they own. If you stop using them they can turn off the links and take the site back.

They could even rent it to a competitor, which would mean that you would have paid to develop your competitor's PageRank.

You will find that any reputable company or specialist will not mind these questions and you will not offend them by asking. If people react badly to these questions then it is not a good sign and I would suggest you carry on searching for an alternative company.

Beware

If you're not convinced about a company or specialist then keep looking.

Getting free advice and help

There are many ways to get further help and advice on your particular area of need but the most effective of these methods is through forums.

An internet forum is an online resource where people come together to hold conversations and ask and answer questions.

It can sometimes seem a difficult task to get answers to your specific questions but with forums it's easy.

Forums often operate like an online community where people can come together and meet to discuss similar topics with each other.

Forum benefits

- It is normally free to join a forum and remain a member
- The forum will be on your desired subject
- It is a fast way to get free answers to your specific questions
- There is usually a friendly and easy-to-use interface
- The people on the forum will range from people with no knowledge to specialists in the field
- You can create incoming links to your site through your own customized signature

There are many forums on search engine optimization but the most effective ones I have found are:

- http://www.webworkshop.net/seoforum/index.php
- http://forums.seochat.com/
- http://forums.searchenginewatch.com/

To get going on a forum you will simply need to navigate to it and select the "create a new account" option.

From there you will need to enter your relevant details and create your account. Once you have done this you can start chatting and asking questions.

Hot tip

Forums will help you increase your knowledge and inward links at the same time.

Beware

Do not attempt to spam or over-sell yourself on your forum or you will become very unpopular and end up getting banned.

180

Google's sandbox

The Google sandbox is a concept that has been coined to describe the effect that new websites have in Google's search results.

New websites do not behave in the same way in Google's search results as older, more established websites.

It seems that Google is less inclined to rank newer websites until they have proved themselves and gone through a probationary period. This seems to be a period of between 90 and 120 days.

This is not to say that everything you do is pointless within this time, it just means that your efforts will probably be put on hold until this period has passed.

The Google sandbox could be used by Google for many things other than just new websites. Google could also use this for websites that it believes are not playing fair or that have suddenly gained large numbers of inward links.

If you have a new website you should make your changes and optimize your website gradually. This includes building links to your website.

You should try to build links slowly over time instead of adding a hundred in one sitting. This sudden spike of inward links could cause you problems. It would look unnatural, as links are not normally achieved this fast.

There are several ways you can deal with the Google sandbox and its effects, including:

- Use an existing, older domain name instead of buying a new one

- Build links slowly over time

- Optimize your website slowly

- In the early days, concentrate on other search engines

- Utilize pay per click (PPC) for your initial placements

The Google sandbox effect is not a recognized algorithm by Google; it is just a phrase to describe the effect often seen with new websites that have only recently been found by Google.

Hot tip

Be patient with new websites as they will need time to mature before Google will rank them at their full potential.

Beware

Do not build links too quickly with a new website as it will look unnatural to Google.

Google's trustrank

Google's trustrank is an algorithm believed to be used to assess how trustworthy your website is in order to improve the effectiveness and relevance of Google's search results further.

There are many things that could effect your trustrank including:

- Domain age
- Number of links you have
- PageRank of the websites that link to you
- Trustrank of the sites that link to you
- Bad topics such as gambling or pornography
- Spam on your site or sites that link to you
- Length of time you register a domain for
- Updating regularly
- Unique IP address
- Displaying a privacy policy
- Displaying contact details including an address
- Sitemaps
- Security (SSL) certificates

The main factors that will probably influence your trustrank are the age of your domain and the quality of the websites that are linking to you.

The main point to remember with both trustrank and PageRank is to ensure everything you do is for the right reasons and that it is ethical.

If you make sure you are not doing anything that you believe could be interpreted as bad practice then the chances are your website will be fine.

Google's trustrank is not recognized by Google as an existing algorithm; it is just a phrase to describe an effect often seen in practice.

Hot tip

Try to get links from well-respected websites like the BBC and CNN as this will help Google to see your website as trustworthy.

Absolute Link
A complete URL that contains the domain name and extension of a website – normally used when linking to other sites.

Accessibility
The extent to which a website can easily be accessed by disabled people and also by search engines.

AdWords
A form of sponsored advertising on Google using pay-per-click ads to generate targeted traffic to your website.

Algorithm (Google's)
Google's secret set of criteria that it uses to analyze your website and define its search engine ranking position.

Alt tags
Strings of text that are used to describe the images on websites to the search engines and screen readers.

Anchor text
Text on a web page that contains a hyperlink redirecting you to another page.

Article
A document used to relay information to its readers, and normally distributed and displayed on other related websites in exchange for a link to your website.

Backwards link
Links from other relevant websites to your website, for which no return link has to be provided.

Black hat SEO
Unethical methods of search engine optimization.

Blog
An online journal used to post thoughts, commentary and news on a particular subject.

Browser
The program used to access and view websites. Examples include Internet Explorer, Firefox, Safari, and Opera.

Cached page
Google's stored copy of a web page.

Campaign
A group of AdWords ad groups in your Google AdWords PPC account.

Cascading style sheet (CSS)
An external style sheet used to store the structure and formatting of your web pages.

Cloaking
A black-hat SEO technique where your website content displayed to a search engine spider is different from the content presented to the users.

Content
The information and data provided on your website in its main body area.

Conversion rate
The percentage of traffic viewing your website that then leads to a sale or similar action.

CPC
The maximum cost per click you will pay when your ad is clicked on.

CTR
The percentage of time your ad is clicked on compared to how often it is shown.

Directory
A website displaying a list of other websites that are grouped into specific categories.

Domain name
The name of your website, for example www.ineasysteps.com

Doorway page
A page created for spamming search engine indexes with the purpose of redirecting you to another page when a particular search phrase is used.

Dreamweaver
A program used to design and edit web pages.

Dynamic website
A site where the content is created dynamically from a database instead of being stored in static web pages.

External links
Links to other websites from your own website.

Flash
Technology that uses a free plug-in to allow your browser to display animations and flash movies as you navigate the web.

Form
Used to collect information from your visitors and send it to a specified predetermined location.

Forum
A facility on the internet used to hold discussions and post information regarding a specific topic.

Frames
Outdated technology used to create websites.

Froogle
A product search engine that displays photographs of products for sale related to your specific search query.

Guestbook
A logging system that allows people visiting your website to leave a public comment.

Header tags
Used to format the text sizing on web pages to help add structure and outline the main section headings.

Home page
The main page on your website, also known as the index or default page.

Hosting provider
A company that provides space on its server to enable you to make your website accessible to all on the World Wide Web.

HTML Hyperlink
Part of a web page that when clicked on will display a different page, the address of which is specified in the link.

Internal links
Links that are placed on a website and used to navigate around it.

Keywords
The words and search phrases targeted when optimizing your website.

Landing page
The page to which you have designed an ad to deliver your visitors.

Latent semantic indexing
Technology used to determine words that are related, to help build relevance.

Link farm
A large number of websites that all link to each other for the purpose of spamming the search engines.

Meta description
The description you have provided in your website to be shown in the search engines.

Meta tags
The tags you have used to describe your website to the search engines.

Meta title
The tag shown in the search engine advert to describe your website and also shown at the top of the page.

Natural listings
The results in Google where the free "organic" search results are displayed.

Off-the-page optimization
The optimization of backward links and of what other websites are saying about your site.

Online competition
The top listed websites for your chosen keywords.

On-the-page optimization
The optimization of your website's content and structure.

Organic search
See Natural listings.

PageRank
A score that Google gives your web page depending on the quantity and quality of your inward links.

PPC (sponsored listing)
Pay per click: the area in Google used to display paid listings.

Reciprocal link
When you link to another website and they link back to your site.

Redirect
When one web page is set up to direct its visitors straight to another page.

Relative link
A link that does not contain the website domain in the address, as it is relative to where it is located.

Resource page
A page where you will place related links to other relevant websites.

Root folder
The main folder on your web server. This will be where your home page is located.

Sandbox
The effects seen with new websites in Google's search results.

Screen readers
A program that presents web content to visitors who cannot see it.

SEO
Search engine optimization, the process of optimizing your website to appear in a better position within the natural search engine listings.

Search engine spider
The robot that Google sends out to crawl the web by going from website to website via links.

Server
The place where your website is stored online and to which you will upload your changes.

Sitemap
A page on your website that includes a list of all of the pages on your site, to enable good navigation.

Site submission
The submission of your website to the search engines.

Source code
The code used to create your website, which is also analyzed by the search engines.

Spamming
Any technique used to falsely improve a website's position in the search engine listings.

Split testing
The testing of ads or landing pages against each other to increase efficiency.

Static website
A website that is updated manually via the use of software or HTML.

Traffic
The numbers of visitors and search engine spiders reaching your website over a given amount of time.

Typo spam
The use of misspelt keywords and/or domain names to canvass lost traffic.

URL
Uniform resource locator. The address of a page on a website that identifies it on the World Wide Web.

Validation
The process of ensuring that a website conforms to the rules and guidelines laid out to ensure its accessibility to disabled visitors.

W3C
The World Wide Web Consortium where the rules and guidelines for accessibility are agreed.

Web ceo
Software used to help analyze and optimize your website and check your rankings.

Website structure
The layout and structure of your website's pages, files and folders.

Website theme
The main focus of your website's content.

M

N

O

P